MARRY ME

MARRY ME

A very funny proposal by
CAREY MARX

headline
review

First published in Great Britain in 2006
by Headline Review
An imprint of Headline Book Publishing

1

ISBN 0 7553 1458 1

Cataloguing in Publication Data is available from the British Library

Typeset in Walbaum by Avon DataSet Ltd, Bidford on Avon, Warwickshire

Printed and bound in Great Britain by Clays Ltd, St Ives plc

Headline's policy is to use papers that are natural, renewable and
recyclable products and made from wood grown in sustainable forests.
The logging and manufacturing processes are expected to conform
to the environmental regulations of the country of origin.

HEADLINE BOOK PUBLISHING
A division of Hodder Headline
338 Euston Road
London NW1 3BH

Every effort has been made to fulfil requirements with regard to
reproducing copyright material. The author and publisher will be glad
to rectify any omissions at the earliest opportunity.

www.headline.co.uk
www.hodderheadline.com

ACKNOWLEDGEMENTS

Special thanks to my writer friend Sarah Morgan, who spent twelve hours without breaks, eating only biscuits, helping me edit the book before I handed it in. When I say she was helping me edit, she was largely ordering me to remove pieces. She also forced sincerity out of me when I didn't think I had it in me and added some humour that had us both giggling over our biscuits. She advised on female perspective, which I have to admit surprised me a few times. For example, I wrote a number of emails to a girl on an internet dating site who claimed to be mad. In my first email I offered to go mad so that she'd like me. She didn't reply. So I wrote more. Eventually I just wrote gobbledegook. I thought it was all very funny, but Sarah gently explained that I was harassing the girl.

These people became zombies to try and help me woo a girl: Jason John Whitehead, Paul Byrne, Kirsty Newton, Nick Doody, Matt Kirshen, Carol Smith, Megan Turner, Richard Phillips and Papa CJ.

These people agreed to be murdered so that I could woo a girl: Martina Messing, Graham Faost, Rob Heeney, Megan Turner, Matt Kirshen, Richard Lester, Dave Bourn, Kieli Smith, Ben Bibbings, Nick and Eva Doody, Sarah Morgan and Monique O'Brien.

I would also like to thank Sony because they gave me a free camera, and Nandos Restaurants because they gave me free chicken and wine for my dates.

Jeff Cohen is an American who carried out his own search for a wife, found one, and has now become a dating expert with his own internet site called www.dating.about.com.

I cannot possibly mention all the people who went out of their way to help me this year. Some are mentioned in the story. But my mission would have been impossible without the abundant assistance I received from the following people: Phil Nichol, Nick and Eva Doody, Matt Kirshen, David Angel, Mark Taylor, Tommy and Trudy Stade, Stephen K. Amos, David Bourn, Barry Castagnola, Brendon Burns, Paul Byrne, Janice Phayre, Chris Gilbert, Jeremy O'Donnel, Steve of France, Richard Phillips, Christian Knowles, Misha Crosby, Simon Trewin, Debi Allen, Noam Friedlander, Helen Simpson, and all at Headline, especially Emma Tait and Wendy McCance.

Finally, of course, all the girls.

FOREWORD

It was a mess. In January it was an idea. In February it became an official quest. Over the next six months I performed 130 gigs, had 120 dates, wrote over 1,000 emails, wrote and performed a show about it all, wrote this book, made lots of friends, upset a few people, proposed marriage several times and ate 50 Chinese meals.

My quest was a mess because it could only ever have been a mess. It was, at times, as quixotic as fastening a belt around a cloud, as frustrating as ironing snow, as pointless as boredom in a dream. But it was also as satisfying as watching a snake charmer get bitten by his snake.

It was a mission which provoked suspicion, anger, encouragement, humour and, surprisingly, romance. If I were to do it all again, I would do much of it differently. Still, I'm really happy about how it ended.

I've changed some names to protect the innocent. More often, I've changed names to protect the not-so-innocent. Most of the names, however, are genuine. All emails are printed with the explicit permission of their authors. I've heavily disguised some characters (I stopped short of giving them moustaches and beards). I've also, at some points, had to combine several events into one to save you from the same confused and desperate multitasking that my social life spiralled into.

If you dated me this year and you think I've written something nasty about you, it probably wasn't you.

Truth is, this has been a difficult story to tell. I've had to take into account many concerns by the potential wives involved over what I might write about them. Some who have seen the book even became upset by what I had written about other women ('How come you said she was beautiful but you didn't say it about me?' etc). One was upset about everything I wrote about her, and eventually I took her out of the book. Then she was even more upset when I told her she had been removed.

That paragraph is a complaint about the task and not a complaint about women. Any criticism of a woman in this book represents my personal point of view about that woman and should not be taken as a criticism of women. You may find me opinionated at times but I hope that overall this work is a tribute to the many fabulous women I met. That is certainly how I feel about it.

I've chosen dates and events that represent the ongoing mood, so many great dates have had to be left out. Sorry.

To see photographs of some people who appear in this story, including the zombies, or for further information on the show, please log on to www.marryme2005.com.

It may have started frivolously, but it became the most intense thing I've ever done. It bashed, battered and buttered my confidence. Yes, buttered. In hindsight, it was enormously enjoyable. It was also a bloody nightmare.

Dedication

As agreed, I will not write your name here. You know who you are.
I love you. Thank you.

2005: The Year of Bold

Standing next to a mountain makes you feel small.
Standing on a mountain makes you feel big.

A resplendent horse-drawn carriage trots and rolls through snowfall along a snow-covered road, jingling its bells as people stand aside. The carriage is overtaken by a little electric car. Other electric cars appear and turn left past the church, past the graveyard of mountaineers who wanted to be high off the ground but ended up under it. The electric cars rattle up the hill between quaint shops, winter-clothing-wrapped people and old wooden huts on stilts. To the right is a sight that inspires legitimate use of a word my North American friends regularly de-power; they use it to describe a half-decent cheese sandwich; they waste it on a dinner invitation; they offer it in response to mildly good news. The word is 'awesome'. The sight is the Matterhorn.

The Matterhorn is a man's man of a mountain. The first time I saw it was in 2004 after three days of disappointing cloud and mist cover. Then one morning I woke up in the hills of Zermatt, Switzerland, and looked out to see the air had cleared to reveal the famous mountain. It was, truly, awesome. The peak looked like the neck of a bodybuilder whose head had been twisted and ripped away. Below this brawny neck, the mountain stretched out horizontally, showing off its broad shoulders, and the dizzying image of the headless hero was complemented by a hirsute display of fir trees running thickly down the mountain's chest. Seen from another angle, the mountaintop is a triangle; the triangle that launched the Toblerone chocolate bar. Even among the experienced, the 4,478-metre peak is considered a difficult climb. Every summer around ten people lose their lives attempting it.

Today, 2 January 2005, I am standing on the summit of the Matterhorn feeling quite relaxed and fairly unfazed by the climb. That is because I'm not on *that* Matterhorn. I'm on the Klein Matterhorn, a ski hill I have climbed by cable car. (It was still a bit scary, though.)

The Klein Matterhorn, 3,882 metres high, is reached by the highest cable car in Europe. On the way up, I made a lame attempt at chatting up a skier who told me she'd come to Zermatt to ride the famous run into Cervinia. It's hard to be sincere when you're chatting up a girl wearing a helmet, goggles, face protector and numerous layers of clothing. She could be skinny, fat, pretty, ugly or male. I knew only that she was about my height and sounded female, so she could have been beautiful for all I knew. As the throng forced its way out of the cable car I realised I'd lost my companions, Craig and Jane, and while realising I'd lost my companions I lost the beautiful/ugly girl/man.

I carry my snowboard through a tunnel to the other side of the peak and to the start of the Cervinia run. I've heard plenty about this run. I've heard that it's seven miles long. I've also heard that it's twenty miles long. And fifteen miles. And twenty-five miles. I've heard it takes an hour of cable cars to get back to the top. And four hours. Craig and Jane are waiting for me, bindings on and ready to ride; we agree to meet at the first good stopping point and I watch them slide away on their boards.

I light a cigarette and smoke it while fixing my bindings.

It's very early in the morning and normally I'm no fan of the concept of morning, let alone early. They say the early bird catches the worm, but they pay no heed to the lesson of the early worm that should have stayed in bed.

2005 is to be a busy, eventful, effort-propelled year. 2004 was to be a lazy pressure-free year, and I'd achieved that admirably. I gigged in '04. I wrote a novel in '04. But I did it all at my own leisurely pace, unencumbered by stress. I decided to go nowhere near the Edinburgh Festival and I decided to say no to any form of disagreeable hard work or commitment. I made the resolution as a present to myself and I'd kept to the plan with a relaxed, smiley ease and many content uses of the word 'no'.

I pull the laces on my boots tight and knot them.

The plan for this year is to pay for my year of lying low. 2005 is the year of bold. A stick-the-neck-out year. When you stick your neck out you may get your head chopped off, or someone might put a sweet in your mouth.

I put on my gloves.

My plan isn't very comprehensive because I haven't yet thought it through, or even taken it seriously. But it is amusing me and sometimes that's enough. This year I'm going to find my ideal woman. And I'm going to marry her. Riding the unknown-length run into Italy will be a dynamic opening to '05.

I fix the chinstrap of my helmet.

2005 is the year of bold. Don't ask, don't get.

I snap my goggles into place.

I am feeling on top form, on top of my game, on top of the world. This year I will achieve amazing things.

I jump the snowboard into position, aiming directly down the mountain. I lean my weight forward, and with a deft whip-like swish of the snowboard I charge down the mountain – for about quarter of a mile, at which point a skier smashes into me, wipes me out and I get airlifted to a hospital.

End of 2004:
The Sperm of an Idea

The Edinburgh Festival is a mammoth event. It's a comedy festival, a
music festival, a dance festival, a book festival, a children's festival, a
theatre festival, a television festival and a street performance festival
all in one city. It's even a bums' festival, I think. I've noticed when I
travel to Edinburgh out of Festival time that there are a few bums
hanging around. Once the Festival starts, there are hundreds of
them. They come from all over Britain for the chance to show off
their new begging lines to huge crowds of tourists, to drink and
exchange stories with other bums, and perhaps to be spotted by the
Head Bum, who invites them to come and beg at other festivals round
the world.

At the end of my self-imposed hassle-free 2004, I considered
going back to Edinburgh to perform another show. I wrote out four
possible ideas, each of which would have made a decent show and
would not have ended up with me getting married. Then, more
because five seemed a better number of options than four, I wrote an
option five on the page: Marry Me.

I had no idea what this show would entail other than me getting married, and I tackled that uncertainty by not thinking about it. Next, I put my ideas through the 'friends process', inviting each of them to consider my four show suggestions and have a giggle with me at the fifth suggestion, which was there for light entertainment.

Every friend picked up on the Marry Me show. On a car journey to a gig, I told my friend David my ideas. He nodded and gave semi-enthusiastic responses. Then I told him about Marry Me.

'What is it?' he asked, animated and already interested.

'I guess it's a show in which I get married.'

'That's great!'

'Is it?'

'Yes.' He was unequivocal. 'How would it work?'

'I don't know,' I said, thinking I should tell him again about the brain idea. I was planning to have the audience walk into a venue made to look like the inside of a brain. The show would be a cerebral look at the cutting-edge discoveries in neuroscience. 'I think I'll advertise for a wife and see what happens.'

He started making suggestions without asking or apparently having any interest in whether I actually wished to be married to a virtual stranger or indeed to anyone at all. He thought it would be funny if the rule stated that I had to marry by the end of the Festival.

'I could end up marrying an ogre,' I protested.

Laughing, he agreed that that would be very funny. Whom he was agreeing with, I was not sure.

I have a friend called Phil, with whom I've shared three different houses over a period of seven years. Phil has a sharp aesthetic eye for art and nature and always has at least a hundred projects on the go at any one time. He has so much energy that if you press down on his head and then let go he will bounce for about three hours.

He listened to my list of ideas and quizzed me about the Marry

Me concept. I guessed answers and managed to achieve vagueness. We talked for an hour over a steak. I started telling him about my idea for a different show, which would take an in-depth look at the sociological uses of humour.

'It will be about how humour is used to drive political campaigns; how money-based Jewish jokes first developed around the time of the Rothschilds' banking dynasty and how Stupid Irishman jokes date from when the Irish Troubles began,' I explained.

'What if nobody wants to marry you?' he asked.

'Exactly. That idea's too risky. The show about humour, on the other hand, could be fascinating. I'm going to research how humour has been employed in desperate human situations. I'll talk to survivors of atrocities. I want to argue a case that humour is a last bastion of human pride.'

'Would you actually get married in the show?'

Other friends' reactions: 'It's great.' 'Do that one.' 'Get married.' 'It's a brilliant idea.' 'Definitely that one.' 'Amazing.' 'Genius.'

I'm easily influenced, which I know to be true because a total stranger once told me that I'm easily influenced and I still believe him. Sometimes people pronounce my name wrongly. They call me Kerry, Corey, Carry, or Kiery, and there is normally a brief moment when I get embarrassed and think I've been pronouncing my name wrongly all my life.

When an idea elicits so much approval, it's hard not to run with it and see where it goes. The idea ran ahead of my mouth during a dinner with my family.

'I'm getting married at the Edinburgh Festival next year, just because it might make a good show,' I heard myself telling them.

None of them batted an eyelid because they all suffer from knowing me too well. 'Sounds like it would make a good show,' they all agreed.

I was very disappointed in them.

One thing I knew for certain, however, was that all sensible women would react against my idea and tell me that it was pathetic and I should grow up.

The Egg of an Idea

'You should definitely do it. Find your ideal partner and marry her. It's so romantic,' said the first female friend I mentioned the idea to.

I started telling every woman I met. Every single one of them found it romantic.

'Don't you think it's ridiculous that I'm going to get married for this reason?' I asked in one conversation.

'No, it's wonderful and romantic.'

'But there's no telling what I might end up marrying.'

'I'll marry you before that happens. You can keep me as a safeguard in case of emergency.'

Three other women made similar offers.

Then they started making demands.

'I think your safeguard group should have certain powers,' said one of them, 'like we should decide which of the women who apply would be best for you.'

Again the idea was running away from me. Not only did the Marry Me show have legs, but those legs were hyperactive. I decided that I didn't want a safeguard group or anyone else telling me whom I should marry.

The female reaction to the concept was another big dollop of encouragement for a show I was still considering dropping. But how could I drop something so popular? Every man wants to come up with an idea that every woman he meets loves.

JANUARY 2005:
BABY STARTS KICKING

On New Year's Eve I performed in Cardiff. On 1 January I dragged myself and a hangover the size of Wales to the station, took a 7 a.m. train to London, took another train to Luton, took a bus to the airport, took a flight to Geneva, took a train to Zermatt and took an electric car up to a hotel in the hills where I met my friends Craig and Jane.

The next morning I was sitting in the hospital in Zermatt feeling sorry for myself and knowing I wouldn't go ahead with the Marry Me show because I was damaged goods. I had a dislocated shoulder, and damage all along my right arm, chest, stomach and all down the left side of my body to my toes. The only part of me not damaged at all was my head, but my helmet had been crushed. I was upset about that because I'd only bought the helmet the day before, and it cost £100. What a waste of money.

While I waited for the results of an X-ray, I went outside and rang friends back in England. I told them that I couldn't go ahead with this show because it might become 'Crippled Comedian Seeks Wife'. Every one of them reacted in the same way: 'That's a better show!' That had always been the problem with the show: anything that should have scotched the plan in fact improved it.

Back in England I went to a house party where a stranger asked my name.

'Carey,' I said.

'Oh, you're the guy who's getting married,' he said.

I never managed to find out where he'd heard about it.

The next week I had meetings with promotion companies for the Edinburgh Festival who wanted to see a write-up for the show I was intending to perform. Awash in the wave of approval I was receiving with the Marry Me concept, I wrote it up.

MARRY ME
by Carey Marx
The show where you can laugh, applaud and marry the performer

Describing the show, I said I'd start looking for a wife in February, giving me just seven months to achieve something I hadn't even considered in thirty-eight years of existence. I would try every form of wife-hunting available. I thought it would be funny to make myself as eligible as possible in the six months before the festival by learning to cook an exciting dish, quitting smoking, getting fit, learning a romantic poem, dressing better, and taking fighting lessons so that I could protect my wife. I liked the idea of becoming a good husband, even if I failed to find a wife.

My View of Marriage

I was neither for it nor against it. I respected other people indulging
in it for whatever they got out of it. Saying I'd get married for a show
hadn't been a big deal. It was like saying I'd become a member of
Millwall Football Club for a show. Such a membership would mean
something to Millwall supporters but it wouldn't mean anything
to me, so doing it would not offend or even wobble my personal
values.

Like most people's, my first impression of marriage came from
my parents, who were happily, loyally married for thirty-five years.
They were a team, like a comfy pair of shoes. In rain they were
wellingtons, in summer they were sandals, but they were always a
pair. As I grew up, I assumed that I would be a part of something
similar, but at thirty-eight I began to realise that I was just a single
slipper, so in love with the family dog that I didn't realise the other
half of the pair was missing. In this analogy the family dog is my life,
my friends, my career, my guitar, reading, magic tricks, biscuits,
snowboarding and being an aloof man of mystery. I never felt as if I
was missing my other half.

Maybe I should have been concerned with this wife-shaped void in my life but it seemed to be something that other people worry about, like suspicious moles and mortgages.

So far nothing had sufficiently motivated me to find a wife. Could it really take something as perverse as a comedy show to drive me into taking the institution seriously? After all, I always assumed I'd get married some day, and I'm a man who needs a mission. I taught myself to smoke because I knew some great tricks with lit cigarettes. Now I'm a brilliant smoker. Maybe I'd be an incredible husband because I wanted to write the best show I could.

My Love Life

I didn't have one. I'd been in three intense, long-term relationships before the age of thirty-two; I'd been in love and experienced loving someone so much I'd marry her, but it felt like something that happened a long time ago, to a different Carey. I'd slumped into a relationship malaise and become blasé about even trying to find a partner, occasionally just settling for a few nights with some drunk girl I'd met at a gig somewhere.

I'd lost interest in one-night stands because they'd become more work than achievement. Promiscuity seemed to involve more promise than cuity.

I'd lost interest in romance and immersed myself in gigging and writing. I'd become a bit cynical. I didn't know I was cynical but here I was, seriously considering marrying a stranger, because the idea of finding the love of my life, without a really good reason, like a comedy show, seemed absurd. Had I given up on love? Would this be a great way to stick it to the romantics and announce to the world I was merely a clown with an amusing wife?

Maybe I was taking all this too seriously. After all, I only needed to get married to satisfy the audience. I could marry an immigrant who wanted a visa, a mate who was up for a giggle, or I could go to Vegas and marry the first drunk I found outside a wedding chapel. I could get a quickie divorce and meet the girl of my dreams later – she'd understand that I'd been married before, and probably find the whole thing very amusing. But was I missing an opportunity? Was it significant that I was even thinking about this marriage as something more than a prank?

I had a choice to make. Was my task to find the perfect woman, subject her to a series of tests to ascertain her suitability, fall in love, and spend the rest of my life with her? Or was I going to go the 'wacky mission' route, have a series of adventures and wind up marrying the most amusing candidate (thus assuring myself comedic immortality as the Wacky Marriage guy)? Either seemed an equally frightening prospect.

I didn't know which route to take, but, for the sake of the show, the lone slipper that was me had to hop its way forward to its destiny. My mission, though vague, was on.

February:
Going into Labour

My literary agent, Simon, called. 'I have some publishing houses interested in your *Marry Me* show.' I vaguely remembered mentioning the show idea to him. 'I've arranged the first meeting.'

In a cab on the way to the meeting, I had a think about the mission plan I'd try to sell. My funny proposition had snowballed into something real. Did I feel comfortable going into a meeting with a gimmicky idea? Yes. It was a funny idea and I'd get to write that book. I put on my long floppy shoes, adjusted my revolving bow tie, and entered the building with a honk of my horn.

I met Simon in the foyer of Headline publishers and we went up to the meeting. We were led into an office that overlooked London, and I was introduced to Headline's decision-makers: Emma, Georgina and James, who were all extremely friendly.

They asked me about my mission.

'I intend to start looking for a wife in March,' I told them (hoping that they wouldn't point out that the write-up I'd sent them claimed I'd start in February (which had originally been January)).

'We like the idea,' said Emma. 'It's refreshing to hear of a man doing something like this. But what if you fail to get married?'

'Then I'll admit failure and that will be the story. The excitement will come from the possibility that I might succeed against the odds.'

'It's an interesting gimmick,' said James. 'So what's your plan? Find a Russian bride?'

'Actually, I've thought about that,' I said, 'and it's a funny idea, but I want to see if I can do this for real. I want to meet a woman I'll really want to marry. That's my mission.'

I wasn't sure if they'd accept this new premise, because if I didn't meet my ideal partner I wouldn't get married and therefore it would just be a guy going out on dates, which lots of guys are doing and isn't much of a story. The thing that made it different was the deadline: having only until the end of August to find my wife. I decided to sell that feature of my quest.

'If we go ahead with this book,' said Georgina, 'we'll be aiming for it to come out for Valentine's Day next year. It says on this sheet that you intend to give yourself a deadline of the end of August, but it's probably better not to rush it like that, and give yourself longer.'

I couldn't believe what I was hearing. My mission was stronger if I *didn't* have to marry anyone and if I *didn't* have a deadline? Great.

In the taxi on the journey home, I told the driver about the meeting.

'So you're just going to go out on dates and probably not marry anyone by no set date?' he asked, puzzled.

'Yes, that's my mission.'

'Do you think they'll commission you to write a book about you probably not achieving this anything by no particular time?'

'I doubt it.'

'Would you really get married?'

I thought carefully and my answer surprised me. 'Yes. If I actually do meet my ideal partner, why wouldn't I want to hold on to her? If I met my ideal biscuit I'd marry it.'

The Baby Is Born
(I Become a Daddy)

On Valentine's Day, I received an email from Simon to tell me that Headline wanted to go ahead with the deal.

I was elated. I was also disturbed, because this meant the *Marry Me* mission was on. I'd have to do it. I had by this time decided to do it anyway, because I wanted to get married. But now I had to mean both of those things. With the book in the bag and the show on the road, I started telling people that I was looking for a wife. Most of them were married and typical responses were: 'You're kidding! You aren't really going to do it are you?' 'Seriously, don't get married.' 'It's a bad idea.' 'Don't do it.' Where were all these people when I originally sought advice?

By now, however, I was set on the idea.

Mission Statement

I made it clear to everyone that I wanted the right to fail. I would not marry just anyone for the sake of it, simply to claim success. I would dedicate my year to finding my ideal partner. I would try every form of wife-hunting available to me. At best, though it seemed highly improbable, I would meet someone and instantly fall in love. If so, it would be the first time this had ever happened to me. If I met someone I liked and thought worth investigating further, I'd arrange another date, and then another, and get to know her fast. At worst, I'd be able to report on the good and the bad of the singles scene. My next few months would be intense.

Deep down, I knew what would happen. I'd meet lots of nutters and I'd fail to find a wife. The failure would be its own success because it would prove that I wasn't single for want of trying. Whether it was because I was too fussy or too set in my ways, or because all the good ones were taken, I'd sunk into and become quite comfortable with my sad existence, like a computer nerd who long ago gave up trying to kick a football. I would come out of this knowing the reason why I could never find my ideal partner, and I would announce that reason.

On behalf of lonely single people everywhere, I would put the dating scene's head on a block for all to witness. But I would put everything I had into my mission. No one would be able to say that I didn't try my utmost. I would put every ounce of my energy into trying to find a wife. I would be bold.

BEING BOLD:
THE MISSION TO FIND A WIFE

Rosie

Nineteen years old, pretty Rosie giggled warmly at my jokes.
I was on stage at a Monday comedy club called Old Rope that I'd
started with Phil. Rosie was in the audience. It was 14 February.
Valentine's Day.

During his act, a comedian called Rhys mentioned his wife, also
called Rosie. Returning to the stage, I asked the Rosie in the audience
her name. 'Rosie,' she replied.

I pointed out that Rhys was a fine example of how a comedian
and a Rosie could be happily married. I told her I was looking for a
wife and asked if she'd marry me. She laughed, which is only one step
down from a yes.

When you ask someone a question and their reply is one step
down from a yes, you have only to take one step down with your
question because you have found their yes-level. So I asked Rosie if
she'd have a date with me. She said yes.

This first yes was a good omen. My mission would start on

Valentine's Day with me gaining a date with a gorgeous nineteen-year-old.

Committed to my mission, ready to take on the Year of Bold and full of Don't ask, Don't get, I left the club and got sick. I had caught a belligerent bout of flu. I did not have time to be ill; I had a wife to find. I grabbed the phone to ring Rosie and set up the first date of my mission and discovered that I'd lost her number.

Becky

After a gig in Rochester, I chose the most attractive girl in the room and approached her by the bar.

'Hi. I'm looking for a wife. Will you marry me?'

'I'm a lesbian,' she said.

'Is that a no?'

'You're not really looking for a wife?'

'Actually, I am. And I'm writing a book and a show about it. What's your name?'

'Becky. Are you being sincere?'

'Extremely. Is your lesbianism negotiable?'

'OK, I'm not really a lesbian.'

'So will you have a date with me?'

'Yes, but I still don't believe you about any of this.'

I gave her my email address so that she could decide if she wanted to write to me and received an email from her two days later.

WORD-OF-MOUTH WIVES

By mid-February, talk of my mission had spread so fast that on hearing my name total strangers said, 'Oh, you're the guy who's looking for a wife.' Friends and strangers offered possible brides from among people they knew.

Nick and Eva, housemates who'd recently married, told me they knew an American girl who might be interested. Eva is American and talks in adjectives. She told me her friend was so like totally cool and that she'd contact me by email. Several days later, I realised that Eva's friend, Paige, had written to me saying she'd marry me but her email had been thrown in the recycle bin. I retrieved it and read it. She did seem so like totally cool. I wrote back and told her how I had heroically rescued her from the recycle bin. Paige described herself as a JAP, which apparently stands for Jewish American Princess, twenty-six years old, and on a six-year degree course in art history, fine art and photography/film. She is attractive and has a sinful sense of humour and a directness I liked immediately. In her email she asked, 'Do you get a lot of ass being on the road and being funny and moderately attractive?' And she advised, 'You need to so do that show, and set it up so you marry me anyway. I have nice boobs.'

We started writing to each other regularly, and we found a form of mutual humour that worked. It was filthy.

I received an email from my friend Amanda. It seemed she had a potential wife for me. Her brazen message said, 'When can you meet, get drunk, and have sex with my friend, Loki?'

Amanda is not someone who squanders words or sentiments. Her email address starts amandaisunique3@ . . .

I wrote to Loki and asked if she liked biscuits. She said yes. She sounded like a perfect wife. We started a flirty and intriguing correspondence.

At this rate, I'd be married in no time.

While feverish with flu, I sent Paige an email loaded with filthy notions. She didn't reply for three days and I thought maybe I'd misjudged this potential wife. From my sickbed, I concluded that I didn't want to marry a prude who couldn't take my sophisticated sense of humour.

OTHERS' VIEWS ON MARRIAGE

Bill and Agnes put up comedians whenever any of us are staying in Brighton. Agnes hails from Glasgow. This couple can out-drink, out-smoke and out-anything-else any comedian. They are loved by the comedy community. They tease each other mercilessly in the way that best friends can, but have an enviable relationship.

When they married in 1958 in a Birmingham registry office, Agnes was a twenty-one-year-old nurse and Bill was a twenty-three-year-old teacher. Agnes told me that she'd never been with a man before she married. 'I hadn't even been manhandled,' she added. 'Nor had I,' said Bill.

There was something in this tale of innocence that touched me.

Since I'd announced my mission, married people had started sharing their views with me.

My friends Tommy and Trudy told me they'd got married just twelve days after meeting, and he'd been away for much of that time. They've now been married for ten years and have two fabulous kids. The story gave me some confidence that it would be possible to meet a partner whom I'd wish to marry as quickly as I was aiming to. I asked Trudy what she considered the most important aspect of a successful marriage. She answered instantly: trust. Tommy told me he's a big advocate of knowing right away if you love someone. 'Wait too long and you'll break up with anyone,' he said.

At a party, I spoke to a girl called Angela. She told me that marriage had profound meaning to her and couldn't be compared with a long-term relationship — it was a far deeper thing. She also told me that she was a Christian and took marriage very seriously. 'I believe,' she said, 'that divorce is wrong and unacceptable. I am married for life. If I ever really, really, had to separate from Dave I wouldn't be able to divorce. I would have no choice but to kill him.'

I'm sure she was joking but she joked with a straight face; I made a mental note not to marry a Christian. Later, I decided that that was too severe and trimmed it down to a rule that I wouldn't marry Dave's wife.

At the same party, I spoke to Rosie, whom I mentioned before when I used her marriage to help me gain a date with a Rosie whose number I lost. In an age when it's the cool thing to diss marriage, and it seems mandatory for married people to enjoy anti-spouse humour, it was refreshing to hear Rosie talk so openly, honestly and positively about the institution. She told me it felt very different from being in a long-term relationship, even one which was intended to be for life. Making the vows in front of all her friends and family had stamped the union as official and solid. Coming home to a husband felt more secure and substantial than a mere relationship. She expressed her views with such charm that I was deeply impressed.

Later, I talked to her husband, Rhys. He was equally positive and confirmed Rosie's statements, but I think he also thought I was being a bit weird with my interrogation about his marriage because he backed slowly out of the room saying that I was being a bit weird with my interrogation about his marriage. That was before I could ask him about the sex aspect of marriage.

Backstage at a gig, I talked to the compere, Nick, who told me he'd been married for eight years. We started talking about marriage. The other comedian on the bill, Alan, joined in: 'I notice you haven't asked me.' He was referring to his being homosexual. So we discussed the question of gay marriages and I said that I thought it strange that gays would want to be involved in an institution that traditionally does not respect them. Actually, it's quite common for oppressed people to take on their oppressors' belief systems. Black slaves were oppressed by whites. You'd expect them to have risen from such oppression with loathing for all their oppressors' beliefs. But the opposite is true. 'Yes,' said Nick solemnly, 'that's exactly like marriage. It's all about taking on your oppressor's beliefs.'

On a train, a convivial, be-suited stranger became my pal. He told me he'd been married for seven years and was a big fan of marriage. 'You have to know how to work it right,' he said. 'Marriage isn't *one* thing, it's many things. You can mould it into anything you want it to be'. I was captivated by his enthusiasm, and my mission started feeling like a doddle. Enthusiasm is a powerful tool; mix it with hard graft and you can build anything.

Halfway through the journey, he made a phone call to his wife and told her the train had been delayed by two hours, which it hadn't. He nudged me, grinning. Then he made a more amorous call and told a young female voice that he'd bought some time to pop round and see her. What a cad! What a bounder! I was deflated and demotivated. A moment later, he stood up and asked me to watch his seat while he went to the buffet car. I nodded, though I really felt like showing my disappointment in him and saying, 'How do I know you're really going to the buffet car? You've probably got another seat-buddy further up the train.' While he was gone, I went through his case and sliced up his trousers.

Back home, I switched on the computer and found an email from

Paige, which included this: 'And when I go to bed shortly, I will think of you and those "randy" things that you said in your 2nd to last e-mail. That was so the E-mail of the year . . . I even read it to my mom . . . she was very impressed! I think she wants to be in your show. Maybe a threesome . . . gross.'

I was appalled by my potential wife's potty-mouth.

A moment later, I was even more appalled by the discovery that it was March. I still hadn't yet gone on a date, started writing my show, or written a word of the (now commissioned) book. It was becoming so frustrating that whenever anyone told me it was March I denied it and was willing to fight over the issue.

End-of-February Report

I'd gained four potential wives (Rosie, Becky, Paige and Loki), lost one of them (Rosie) and been on no dates. My mood was tentatively excited.

February had largely been lost in sickness, physical pain from my accident, and sixteen gigs in Dubai, Scotland, Ireland and all over England. To compress an adult life of wife-hunting into just a few months, I'd have to become super-efficient and much bolder. I had no idea how to go about doing that, so I slept on it for a few days.

MARCH:
KNOWN POSSIBLE WIVES

I'd repeatedly failed to meet Becky because we kept missing each other's calls. From time to time my phone rang but I could only tell it was Becky by her name coming up on my phone, because all I heard was fuzz. I tried ringing her back but ended up leaving messages, and it was becoming difficult to leave new messages because I soon exhausted all humour about leaving messages replying to her messages replying to my messages.

Jode

I'd first met Jode at the Reading Festival. We hung out and had a great time and romance could have blossomed, except that she decided to move to Prague. I hadn't seen her for two years but thought about her whenever I heard the word 'goulash'.

On 2 March I sent her an email to tell her about my show and to ask if she'd consider marrying me.

Sarah

Slim, cool, easy-going, good to chat to, broad sense of humour, very attractive, has been asked out by most of the men I know, and whenever her name comes up I discover someone else who once asked her out. Sarah and I became friends seven years ago, when she went out with my housemate.

I asked myself why I'd never asked her out, and I couldn't think of a good reason. Now I had the perfect excuse.

I rang her, told her about my mission and then heard myself blurt out, 'Will you go out on a date with me?' An extremely long split second passed before she replied, 'Yes.' I set a date for our date fast, before she could change her mind. I put down the phone and thought this might be the best show idea I'd ever had. I'd take Sarah out, romance her and get everything right, and she'd marry me and we'd both be happy and everyone would be impressed by how efficiently I'd completed my quest. Plus I'd be married to Sarah. A picture of my mission reaching a happy ending formed in my brain and took precedence over the many pictures of unhappy endings.

My mission glimmered with effulgent promises of a fun journey to a joyous ending. My story would be a fairy tale. The mood was happy-go-lucky, and everything was falling into place without too much effort. I would almost certainly marry Sarah. If I didn't, Becky had seemed very cool, so she might turn out to be wife material. If not, the longer shots of Loki and Paige were promising because we were already having good relationships in cyber world. Finding a wife was turning out to be easy.

I received an email from Jode in Prague. She said, 'This marriage thing is definitely an interesting idea and I am well up for being one of the applicants.'

Another great result. Here was a girl whom I'd already got to know, at least a little, and whose company I enjoyed. Her reception of my mission had a jocular air and this delighted me. I only wanted to date girls who were amused by my endeavour.

Sauntering along a street singing 'I'm Getting Married in the Morning', I ran into a friend who said, 'Oh, by the way, Sarah's been trying to contact you but she lost her phone. It's just that I've been dating her.'

I was amused. He's someone I like. Good luck to them.

'I was thinking about getting serious with her,' he said.

Ha! I thought. Typical man. I bet his idea of serious is leaving a toothbrush at her house. I was going to marry her. I would win her back.

In the meantime, however, I needed some more potential wives and decided that a stranger would be best because she would not start going out with my friends the moment my back was turned.

INTERNET DATING SITES

I rang Becky the Uncontactable and got her answering machine. I did not leave a message.

I joined an internet dating site. Through the night every night I wrote emails to try and find my ideal woman. My first contact emails were always silly because that would get a silly response and told me if I had at least found a girl with whom I could get silly, which was a good start. My second email was normally sillier. My third was normally an apology for my second. My fourth was normally a reassurance email concerning the lady's role in the book and show I was writing.

My profile read:

I'm writing a show for the Edinburgh Festival and a commissioned book about my attempt to find myself a wife this year. And I mean it. I am a professional stand-up comedian. I snowboard. I have accidents snowboarding. My favourite food is Shepherd's pie with petit pois and English mustard all mushed together in a way that makes other people feel ill. I play guitar. I have my own rented room. I live in a house of comedians. It's funny (and I want out – it's too funny). I read all kinds of things. I'm unconventional (see comment about Shepherd's pie). I prefer coffee to tea. I hate Marmite but love peanut butter (yes, I'm a peanut-butter-type). If push comes to shove I would rather a cat than a dog, though I hope that I am never forced to make that decision. I used to be a magician and can still pull a coin from your ear. I just did. Tahdah!

I want a girl who looks good in a hat. OK, that's not totally necessary. Your mother should be Irish, even if you are not. We all know how much fun Irish mothers are: they are low maintenance and easily appeased with gin.

The initial responses to my profile involved special offers, investment opportunities, and a few asylum seekers who I think were impressed that I had my own rented room. I spent hours searching through profiles on dating sites. I wanted girls who were unconventional but not nutters, and there turned out to be a thin line between the two.

First, I tried to find a girl who would be compatible with me, or at least who seemed interesting and might be fun to get to know. After a copious amount of squandered correspondence, I became pickier. Most of the ads were bland. Endless numbers of girls 'Like to have a laugh' or 'Enjoy having fun' or 'Would like to meet someone interesting'. What do they think other girls are after? Many had scarcely a whit to say about themselves. Others were too opinionated. I found that grammar and punctuation considerably affected me. Multiple exclamation marks, smiley faces, 'Lol's, and 'Ha ha's littered many of the profiles so much that I lost all desire to talk to their authors. One lady puts 'Lol' (laughs out loud) after every sentence she writes. Multiple exclamation marks are simply not correct. They have no meaning. You either exclaim or do not exclaim. You certainly do not very exclaim.

One girl said she was too shy to put a photo of herself in her profile. I replied saying that I would really like to see a photo. She responded: 'You don't understand. I am REALLY shy. If we go out together a few times and get to know each other, then I will send you a photo.'

Another wrote to tell me she'd fallen in love with me and she included a two-page love poem, written in rhyming couplets, which would have embarrassed most greetings-card manufacturers.

> Our love it has begun
> Like the setting of the Sun
> Oh our love will grow and grow
> And good times we will know
> And always be together
> In every kind of weather
> Our hearts are melded as one
> We shall have daughters or a son
> I want to feel your breath in my ear
> When you're not around I shed a tear
> Your heartbeat is all I need to hear
> To make my heart empty of fear

> Et cetera.

I've paraphrased her poem. This one is a lot better.

One girl had said in her profile that her favourite book was *Don't Sweat the Small Stuff*. In her email to me she asked if I'd read it. I replied that I was not a big fan of the self-help genre. She replied angrily, telling me that the book had helped millions of people and that I was judgemental and arrogant. I replied that she should read the book again.

Some girls dropped me when they found out about the book and the show, because they didn't want their friends or family or someone to know they were on a dating site. One or two became nutters quickly – actually, more than two. One email was from a lady called Susan, who did not have a picture up. In her profile, she claimed to be aged twenty-five and looking for a man aged between forty and ninety-nine. She was a non-smoker but wanted to meet a smoker. Her favourite book was called *How to be Great in Life*. Soon, I thought, I'd have all the evidence I needed to declare a happy failure to my mission. The singles scene and the nutter scene are one.

I wrote to a girl called Danielle, who had much in her profile to recommend her.

I told her that if she married me, I would buy her a bicycle.

She replied saying that bicycle seats 'hurt her arse' and asked if I would buy her a washing machine.

I wrote back:

OK it's a washing machine, and I'll even take you to the shop and make sure you can test them all out to find one that doesn't hurt your arse.

How long have you been on this site, Danielle? And how's it working out for you? How many nutters have you dated? Are you a nutter? If your answer to the last question was yes, please state what type of nutter you are:

a) Aggressive
b) Alien abductee
c) Obsessive sandwich fixation
d) Bunny-boiling stalker
e) Collector of pictures of kettles
f) Think you're a 50-yr-old male dwarf from the Shetland Isles and that it's the year 1862

g) Constantly terrified of sheep even when there are no sheep around

h) Other

If you are a nutter (I couldn't see anything in your profile to suggest you are but I'm new to all this and still slightly suspicious) I would still like to meet you so long as you don't nut it up during our date.

You might have seen from my profile that I'm writing a show and a book about my attempt to find Miss Wonderful this year.

Are you wonderful? I think there's a big chance that you might be and if so that would be even better than if you're a nutter.

I finished by warning her not to push for more than a washing machine.

I wrote to a girl who employed the nickname Meganetta and who'd said she wanted a man who was at least six foot, and also that she hadn't yet met the right man because she was fussy and busy.

No, Meganetta. No no no. The reason you are still single is not that you are simply too fussy or too busy. Absolutely not. Your problem is quite specific. You are looking for a man of the wrong height. A lot of people make this mistake. They are so busy looking up at the pretty blue sky, the gliding clouds, the fluttering birds, the trees and the giraffe heads, that they completely miss a fiver on the pavement. Yes, I am that fiver. And frankly I'm getting a little tired of you stepping on me while you walk around with your head all full of upness. What you need is someone shorter than you. Someone you can look down to. There are many advantages in going out with someone a bit shorter than you. I could wear a table-hat for you to put your drink on while we're walking together in the park. If we are hugging face to face you could kiss the back of my head if you wanted to. Plus, you get to have children of a height between ours who won't have to listen to all those tall jokes (is it snowing up there etc) that you have suffered all your life and that has made you miserable at times. Think of them and their needs.

Carey

Two days later, I received her reply.

Carey

Thanks for your hilarious email! I'm sure you don't need telling that a sense of humour like yours is such a huge turn on – a giggling girl is easy prey! – or maybe it's just me that's easy – I was raised in Essex after all.

And cheers for adding a photo. I've always had a theory that the best-looking screen actors are always the shorter ones (Tom Cruise, Brad Pitt, Johnny Depp . . .) and that's really a bugger if I should ever happen to bump into one of them in a chic London brasserie or a bookshop in Notting Hill and they were to ask me on a date. Anyway, the photo revealed you to be a bit of a cutie too – theory proved correct.

You must not feel that the height problem is caused by your height, rather by mine – you see, I am pretty Germanic in stature (size 10 feet!), tall and big(ish) boned, and I am reduced to tall and willowy when stood beside a man who's a big unit. So despite the fact that our potential children (you boys are always marrying us girls off in your minds from the first moment of meeting), may proffer from this union, I don't want to spend the rest of our married lives feeling like a massive matriarch as I gain several more stone bearing our large family.

Now do you see my rationale?!

Meganetta x

Happy to find out that my emails were funny and that I looked like Brad Pitt, yet disgusted that all boys were trying to get married quickly, when I thought I was unique, I wrote back:

Meganetta

I'm on an internet machine in Debenhams in Cardiff needing a wee and unable to do anything about it because I have no more change on me and can't stop someone using this machine while I search the department store.

Hope you enjoyed that romantic opening to this letter.

I was thinking that one day we could have a big house with a huge garden and trenches running through both so that we can walk around our house and garden holding hands with you in the trench and always appearing the same size as me. Do you have a problem with living in a trench?

Oh no, instead of allaying your fears and showing you how un-height-biased I am, I've just gone on about height again. Sorry. Forgive me. Let's meet and have a fun date anyway and laugh about how unsuitable we are for each other even though we turn out to have all the same hobbies, favourite films, favourite books, and like going to the same places.

Now I'm bursting for that wee. Someone else can have this computer.

Speak soon,

Carey

Internet dating had begun to appeal to me. It was a huge woman-shop. For hours I browsed through all the colours, sizes and shapes that women come in.

Getting Organised

On a rainy day on a boat on the Thames, I met a couple of clever lads called Chris and Jez who can do things with computers.

'I need a website so that women can contact me,' I told them.

'Tell us what you want it to look like,' Chris offered, 'and we'll do what we can.'

'I'm afraid I have no time to help you with my problems. I have a wife to find.'

'Leave it with us,' said Jez.

'That's what I was going to do.' We shook hands and I left.

By the time I returned from Cardiff, they had created a dating site on which the users found that their ideal match was me. As soon as they told me the web address, I started announcing it on stage at every show.

Here is my first contact:

Hey – I saw you at the Komedia in Brighton the other night, and was interested in your marriage proposal. I am technically male, and heterosexual, but if you're up for it I'll marry you – it'll mean we can get all sorts of gay-friendly financial perks for a start, and if you decide you don't like it, you can sue for divorce on the grounds that I refused to consummate the relationship.

Yours sincerely,

Nick

Within a week, I had five more emails, these from ladies who'd seen me on stage. I also had two emails from freelance journalists offering to write articles about my mission. I realised what good soundbites my nutty idea offered. It had gained me a book deal and now it was capturing the imagination of journalists. I decided to see what else it could do, so I wrote to a company that specialises in electrical goods and asked for a digital camera to photograph my dates.

A nice man replied saying that I could have their latest camera. 'Damn,' I thought at this instant success. 'I should have asked for a video camera.' I wrote back cheekily stating that I would be happy to accept the gift as a wedding present but not as sponsorship.

I wrote to a restaurant chain that does good chicken. They agreed to send me vouchers for chicken and wine so that I could take dates to their restaurant.

I rang my comedy agent and told her I wanted less work. I put down the phone wondering if I had really just said that.

All doubt that I would find a wife became extinct. I had a website, a camera, a load of chicken and the enticement of a free bicycle to the girl who marries me. Now, if I knew anything about women it was that they love being photographed eating chicken while riding a bicycle. Unsurprisingly, I immediately had a batch of new offers.

Word of mouth added another three women to my possible-wives list. I had another four numbers from women who'd approached me after gigs during which I'd announced my wife-hunt on stage. I'd joined another five dating sites and opened some promising dialogue

with a few interesting women. I had enough options. It was time to start the dating.

The Year of Bold could not have been going better. I'd stuck my neck out and people were filling my mouth with sweets.

My First Date

I'd only once in my life been on a blind date. I continued dating the girl for a couple of weeks but lost interest in her because she was an extreme depressive who constantly forewarned me of the time I would dump her as all her past boyfriends had. She regularly practised her dumped-demeanour in preparation for this inevitable event.

'You're going to dump me soon,' she'd say when I told her how beautiful she looked in her frumpy jumper. And then her face would droop in bewildered horror and put out the ambience of a hearse. 'I always knew you couldn't love me.'

At least, I thought, when I do end it I know from our rehearsals how she'll react. But I was wrong. The reality was much worse. I met her in a busy pub and told her it wasn't working out. I only managed half the sentence before she exploded with tears and screams. I took her outdoors where she wailed and shuddered so violently that a workman turned off his pneumatic drill to see what all the fuss was about.

Now, many years later, I was about to experience the first date of my mission. Late for this very first date and with a decision in my head that this would not become a trend because I intended to become efficient as part of my becoming eligible, I told the cab driver about my mission. When he replied, I instantly hated his accent. It sounded like a Jamaican accent that had been in an altercation with a steamroller, because it strained with vowels so elongated that some of them lasted a whole street. The reason I hated his accent was because I loved it but knew I wouldn't be able to write it without seeming to make fun of him. But then I thought, What the hell.

'I'm beeeeg fan of marreeeeeej,' he told me, sounding like he was going to turn the word into 'marijuana'. 'What yoooo doiiiiiiiiiiing is a goooooood thing. A goooood thing. Yes it is.'

'Are you married?'

'I am marrieeeeeed.' He nodded thoroughly. 'Marreeeeeej is a gooood thing. Eeeeeet is an honourable thing. Yes it is.'

'How long have you been married?' He was putting me in the mood for my date.

'Diss eeeeees my fourth marreeeeej now. Yes it is. We are not talking now. Biiiiiiiig argument. Not speeeeeak to her for three weeeeks.' He thumped the dashboard and stared hard through the windscreen, clearly upset. By the time we had arrived at our destination he had changed his advice to, 'Never have anyyyyyyting to do weeeeev women.'

Loki

In the pub, there was only one woman sitting alone. She looked anxious. I couldn't tell how old she was, but she had a corrugated face and an expression so contorted that a funny-fairground-mirror could only have improved it. Oh my God! Help! Panic! Fire!

Fortunately, at that point Loki walked in looking good. We are about the same age. She is a good shape and she looks comfortable in it. We went for a meal in a restaurant she had organised. The food was superb. The evening was superb. Everything was superb. But there was one snag.

'What's this wife-hunt thing you mentioned?' she asked as we finished the main course.

'You don't know?'

'No.'

'Amanda didn't tell you?'

'No.'

'What did she tell you?'

'She sent me a text saying, "When are you going to meet, get drunk and have sex with my friend Carey?"'

'Ah. I see.'

'So what's this wife-hunt thing you mentioned?'

It's hard to say to a woman, 'I like you. Will you be one of my potential wives? I'm planning on seeing more women over the next few months than any man you've ever dated before, and then I might marry one of them.'

Fortunately, she found the marriage thing funny. She told me she wasn't the jealous type and that she'd like to see me again. She decided to see me again immediately, and invited me back to her house.

Loki elected to be called Loki in the book. She explained that Loki was the Norse god of mischief.

Loki is very intelligent; she's a wordsmith and has a sharp sense of humour. She has an enviable self-contained lifestyle as a writer working from home in these convenient days of the internet. We agreed to meet for a second date.

I left, thinking the thought of the moment: 'Dating is great fun.' I'd been honest with her and she'd appreciated my honesty. So long as that continued to be the general reaction, I'd find a wife in no time and no one would get hurt in the process.

Getting Unorganised

I called Becky and left a message about how the humour of leaving messages about leaving messages had enervated.

On an Underground train, my phone was stolen. It had on it numbers I'd gained from potential wives, some of whom I'd arranged dates with and was supposed to ring again with the full details. Many of the numbers were irretrievable because I hadn't written them down. I realised that this had happened because I had spent time with Loki, the god of mischief. I am not superstitious (or even slightly stitious) but superstition is sometimes better than its alternative – superblaming yourself.

Paige rang me from America. We were on the phone for about an hour. I said hello. She said hello. And then she talked for that whole time without me managing to slip in more than an occasional word. Fortunately, it was an entertaining speech, but it made my pen dangle over her name on the possible-wife list. If the pen dropped, it wouldn't be adding a tick. She'd clearly had a drink – every few minutes for at least an hour before the call. At the end of the call, she told me she'd enjoyed talking to me and that we must talk more. Part of me thought the only way she could talk more would be if she had an operation to put gills in her neck so she didn't have to breathe through her mouth. I put the pen aside because I did not think it fair to blow her out just yet, and anyway I wasn't in a position to blow anyone out just yet.

Reporting on my marriage progress at the Old Rope comedy club, I told the audience about the girl in America who'd talked non-stop for an hour. A woman in the audience who'd given me her phone number a few weeks earlier came over after the show to chat. I apologised that I had not called her yet because I had been busy. She pointed out that I had talked to one of the other women for an hour. This sticky moment opened my eyes to a glaring problem with my mission: my potential wives would too easily find out everything I was up to by coming to my gigs.

I consider myself to be immensely loyal and honest but there are times when truth is simply unkind. If somebody has something about them which they cannot help but which turns you off, should you tell them? One girl I courted briefly some time ago had a horrible kiss. A kiss and a hug can tell you a lot about your compatibility with someone. That relationship ended quickly because I couldn't face that kiss. But that wasn't the reason I gave her for our break-up.

After the incident at Old Rope, I became aware of the complications that came with my mission. Reporting on my progress in my Edinburgh show, at previews for the show and in a book meant that honesty would be both a necessity and a concern. White lies would be heard by those involved; women I dated would have easy access to information on the other women I was dating. I am quite private, but my private life would have to become mostly public. I had unwittingly traipsed onto a path full of pitfalls, and soon afterwards the gate closed behind me in the forms of a book deal and the signing of Edinburgh contracts. I would have to tread carefully because the way ahead could be as fructuous as it could be blighted.

I spent most of March gigging, writing to women on dating sites and having meetings concerning the mass of things I had to do in order to take my show to the Edinburgh Festival.

A friend advised me to search for women who had similar hobbies to mine. I quite like chess so I went to a chess club, but the club seemed to attract mostly men and the women were mostly men, too.

I turned thirty-nine on a train to a gig in Brighton and came home to London straight after the gig so that I could answer some of the emails from women that were now oozing in from various sources. Most of the writers were amused or impressed by my mission.

Also in my inbox was a message from Sarah. She'd got engaged to my friend.

Ha! I thought. Engaged is not the same as married. I was still far more committed to her than was this pretender she'd got tangled up with. Despite having not spoken to her for several weeks, and despite her being engaged, I still considered her my number-one potential wife.

I went back to Brighton for another gig and returned to London for more meetings, running Old Rope and other gigs. On the dating sites I'd joined, I found a number of replies from promising possible-wives but I hadn't enough time to get back to them all. My solution to the problem was to be a failure. I expect that, like everything, the characteristic of being a failure exists for a reason and is supposed to be employed at times such as this, when it is the most effective form of action.

A new end of mission scenario snapped into existence in my head: I would fail to find a wife and have to admit it was because I am incompetent.

I reminded myself that I had to be bold and make things happen, so I vowed that I would spend all my free time in Southampton at the coming weekend writing.

In Southampton, I worked hard on my palm computer for a few

hours until it crashed. It would not even turn off. So I pressed the Reset button and it reset to the state in which I had first bought it with none of my writing still existent. Instead of crying about it, I boldly went out and found a pay-as-you-go internet machine and worked on that. It crashed. I started again. Toward the end of writing a second email to one girl, the machine demanded more money and then wouldn't accept any. I watched my long email vanish. I went out and found an internet shop and wrote for three bold hours, surrounded by kids playing video games and screaming about their successes to each other. The computer crashed. I called over the assistant, who came once he had finished his video game. He rebooted the machine before I could shout, 'Noooooooooooo,' and it came back on without any of my work. I returned to the hotel and sat on the bed with old-fashioned paper and pen. The pen ran out. I went out to buy a new pen. It started raining and I was only wearing a T-shirt. Soaked, I returned to the hotel and lay on the bed feeling useless at finding a wife, poor at being bold, and not even wanting to, er, touch myself in case anything else broke.

I needed a wife to help me find a wife.

Back home, Becky rang and told me she'd seen a photo of me at a place called the Five Lakes Resort and we could meet for our date there. I told her I had no knowledge of any such gig. Then I darted straight off out to a show, which I made in the nick of time. I'd been told the show was in a place called Tolleshunt Knights in Maldon, Essex. When I arrived I discovered that the venue was the Five Lakes Resort and I actually could have met Becky there. Too late. I tried to call her but there was no answer. The prospect of failing in my mission through incompetence regained its hold over my thoughts.

However, on that calamitous day in Southampton, I did manage to contact the first girl I'd found on the dating sites. Her name was Heather.

CHAPTER HEATHER

When I first joined the internet dating sites, I was struck by how many of the female adverts were hesitant and apologetic. To the question, 'What are you like?' many replied with opening phrases such as, 'Hmmmmmmmm, what am I like? I'll tell you . . .' or 'Tell you what I'm like? . . . I don't know really . . . well, I'll have a go . . .' or 'I can't really think of anything but I'll try. Some people tell me I'm . . .' Et cetera.

Other adverts had claims of great beauty and grandeur.

I wrote to a few girls, among them Heather. She seemed more assertive than those first examples without being an egoist, and had an interesting profile. She replied saying that she liked my email and gave me her personal email address.

She had style. In her profile her answers to the question, 'What things could you not live without?' included pesto and a dog, though she admitted in brackets that she hadn't got a dog.

I wrote to her personal email address from my personal email address:

Heather

We have now progressed to the personal email level of a relationship. It already feels more intimate. Imagine scented candles around your computer; everyone else is out; a gentle African drum beat can be heard from somewhere off in the distance; your chair becomes a water-chair (like a waterbed but still a chair); a red/blue/green cocktail appears in front of you – you have a sip. It's delicious. A little puppy with the floppiest ears and the biggest cutest brown eyes that you have ever seen jumps up and nestles into your lap. You see from his collar that he is called Pesto.

By now, you either slip your shoes off and relax back into your chair, or you think, 'This guy's a bit of a smoothie-git.' Hopefully, your shoes are off. If instead you're thinking I'm a smoothie-git then you're only right in as much as I'm being a smoothie-git to amuse you and not because I'm a real smoothie-git. OK, now that's sorted out, let's go back to imagining that you are taking this, our first intimate email, seriously.

You're sitting back in your chair, relaxed almost to the point that if a friend saw you now he or she might ask if you're OK and say that you're acting a bit weird; all possible distractions in the form of people and commitments have been exterminated; you don't need a wee (damn, shouldn't have put that thought in your head. See, I'd never make a real smoothie-git); you can feel your heart speeding up a little as if it's trying to tell you that maybe this is someone you'll be waking up with some day soon and not wanting to untangle yourself from and knowing from the secure, sensual warmth of his touch that it's mutual. You think it's getting a bit hot and that you should turn the heating down. Don't do it, Heather. It's not the heating. Ho no. It's you. Your personal thermostat is going through the roof as your imagination boils and bubbles with romantic longings of a kind you have never felt before and did not know you were capable of. You throw your head back, spraying sweat from your now soaking hair, and you scream a name, and that name is Pesto.

Pesto? PESTO? Damn it, Heather, I bought you that imaginary doggie as a present so that you would get to know ME. And instead this happens. The dog would never have turned your chair into a water-chair. I did that.

Heartbroken, I get up to leave. As I reach the door, I look you in the eye and smile slightly, and I look at Pesto and nod knowingly, and in a broken but gallant voice I wish you both a good life together. I close the door behind me quietly and am never seen again.

You laugh. You open a cupboard and put Pesto in with the other imaginary pets that men on the dating site have bought you. You laugh again.

A few days later, I received a reply. She started:

Carey dear Carey – what a breath of fresh air you bring/are.

I did try to follow your instructions to the attached, but while I would dearly have loved to first greet you surrounded by the lilting sounds of African drums (is THAT romantic? – maybe your ex-partner, the Masai princess, still brings tears to your eyes; if so, must get out me Guiro and Claves . . . memories of Music class in Primary school) (take a deep breath now and I WILL finish this sentence) . . . sadly I'm in the office in a POD (such a strange biological, almost organic, use of a word for something which is in fact a desk for commercial output = less organic) . . . I DID find myself being slowly drawn to the screen as I read your words though AND smiling.

She also said that a friend of hers who'd been involved with the comedy business knew of me and had said good things, and she finished with a PS telling me that Pesto the dog liked me.

Back in London, I had another email from her, which ended with the sad news that Pesto had got sundried over the weekend. I had no idea what sundried meant but felt that it must be a bad thing and that he was probably dead. I wrote back with condolences.

I'm heartbroken about Pesto. He had such a short non-existent life and I know his imaginary friends will miss him as we do. He went through life thinking that he was nothing and being right about that. He wished only to be able to wish and he wished that every bone he buried was a wish bone, which is strange because just a moment ago he only wished to be able to wish and yet he apparently also wished that bones were wish bones and that is impossible. But such was the mystery of Pesto.

She wrote back:

Pesto was only Sundried not smothered – he's cooling off in the fridge (wrapped in a hot water bottle for now and left a rather juicy bone for him to freeze with ... I mean chomp on) ... fear not :) he WILL return

Which was a relief, but left me feeling a bit stupid for thinking he was dead. I told her I was relieved that Pesto was OK and invited him on our date.

I suggested that she didn't stand next to any other redheaded women when I arrived to meet her. In her reply, she wrote,

I was going to withhold the following and see what happened on Wednesday, but that would give me an unfair advantage ... Anyway Carey – I'm not a red-head. The pic does make me appear as one I guess but thought it only fair to let you know ... so you won't now be expecting Rula Lenska's 2nd cousin and then I rock up with my pink Mohawk, I mean, blonde hair.

That said, in my mind's eye I shall be expecting you to be wearing what your photo portrays and leaning against a tree.

Well, her photo had made her look like a redhead. Now, I was not at all sure what she would look like. So, I wrote again suggesting we employ the following code when we approached each other.

Heather: I hear the sun shines over Dover on this glorious day.

Carey: Indeed, it would be a good day to travel to Calais.

Heather: Yes, Calais, oh Calais, oh wonderful Calais.

Carey: Hmmmmmm . . .

Both then sing the chorus to 'Bat out of Hell' by Meatloaf.

After memorising the code she was to eat her computer.

We arranged to meet in a pub in Leicester Square. En route, I sent her a text message saying that if we could arrange to meet half an hour later than planned, I wouldn't have to make a bad impression by arriving late for our first date. I'd intended to take along a present, but my tardiness made it impossible. I considered grabbing a dog biscuit for Pesto as I passed a pet store, but decided against because I didn't know how a girl I'd never met would react to being given a dog biscuit.

I arrived early under the new timetable and spent fifteen minutes in the pub waiting for Heather, watching the door and watching unattractive, elderly, saggy, scary, bizarre possible-Heathers passing by the window. One possible-Heather had a nose so large that I cannot believe there are any photos of her in which her face and the tip of her nose are both in focus. There is a certain frisson in the date-waiting moment. I love a good frisson. Sometimes I can even enjoy the frisson that comes just before an expected frisson.

An attractive possible-Heather walked into the pub and turned out to be Heather.

We chatted easily over a drink and then meandered through Covent Garden and had a meal in a Mediterranean restaurant. At some point during the downing of a couple of bottles of wine, Heather presented me with a kazoo that she had bought me as a gift. Whilst toying with the kazoo, I broke it, but still managed to get some kind of noise out of it, which I was now drunk enough to believe that everyone else in the restaurant was enjoying. The kazoo had come in an envelope on which Heather had thoughtfully made a cut-out representation of Pesto the dog. I wished I had bought her the dog biscuit.

As we got drunker, Heather demonstrated her ability to whistle the sound of a spaceship landing. It sounded exactly like a spaceship landing, I think. Then she demonstrated a spaceship taking off. Next she attempted a spaceship going berserk, which was again very impressive and certainly one of the skills that I would expect my wife to have.

We were sitting by the stairs in the upstairs part of the restaurant and as people left, I thanked them for coming.

'We had a lovely meal, thank you,' said an amiable elderly lady.

'Do you own the restaurant?' asked her husband.

Of course I told them that we did.

'How long have you owned it?' said the lady.

I turned to Heather for advice, and keeping an admirably straight face she informed them, 'Fifteen years.' I almost believed her.

'We were just talking about when we first used to come here and you offered a three-course meal for five pounds.'

'Oh, yes, I remember that,' I said.

'It must have been before your time here.'

'Yes, I meant I remember the last owners telling me about it.'

'Well, it's been lovely,' they told us as they left.

'Do come again.'

Heather and I left shortly afterwards and drifted off to find more nightlife. We went to a slot-machine shop and played a game of pool, and then moved on to a nightclub, but it was closing. A heavily built heavily drunken South African man in a rugby shirt was just leaving the club. We adopted him and went on to another club, which would not let us in because we had a heavily built heavily drunken South African man in a rugby shirt with us. We found another club which was happy to the point of delirium to take our money. Heather and I found a quiet dark booth where we drank, talked and kissed. She told me she felt comfortable with me. I reciprocated. She told me she felt uncomfortable that I would be doing this with lots of other girls.

'Marry me now, then,' I said. 'Then I won't need any more potential wives.'

I meant it sincerely but it came out somewhere between creepy and threatening.

Trying to ease the moment, I said, 'There's no hurry. We have all the time in the world until August.'

Then I realised my watch was missing. A bouncer told me far too quickly that it hadn't been handed in.

Quite sozzled, we slipped out of the club and walked to a cab rank, where we kissed until it was time to say goodnight. We exchanged text messages on the way home and the sweetness of her kisses loitered alluringly in my mouth.

While we were in the restaurant, she'd asked if she could have her own chapter in the book I was writing. I told her that she could and that it would be called 'Chapter Heather'. She said it wasn't really necessary, and she'd been joking.

A MAN CALLED
JEFF COHEN

On the internet, I found the site of an American man called Jeff Cohen.

> When Jeff Cohen wanted to find a wife, he set up a dating program including 77 blind dates, 3 trips to Club Med, one dating service gold membership, 4 Hamptons summer shares and one Jersey Shore house, and 300 nights in NY & NJ bars ogling, flirting, and in some cases leaving with phone numbers scribbled on napkins. Mr. Cohen's dating passion helped him find his wife and also establish a company aimed at teaching individuals to reach their human potential in love, career, family, & friendships.

Apparently he met his wife on the seventy-eighth date, and now uses his experience to help others, through his website. I wrote to him, asking for advice specifically on how to avoid anyone getting hurt. My date with Heather had brought home the realisation that it wasn't just me in this experiment.

In his reply, Jeff wrote:

I think the key for you in meeting lots of women is to be clear that you are truly looking to get married, so you're not wasting anyone's time. If in fact you truly hit it off with someone, you'll walk down the aisle. At the same time, be honest, and as soon as you realize you're not with the right one, tell her, and move on. She'll appreciate the honesty.

I had a problem with that advice. I wasn't just truly looking to get married. I was truly looking to see if I could find my ideal partner, in which case I would marry her. It is a subtle but crucial difference. I didn't want to be married for the sake of being called 'husband'. I wanted to marry someone only if I could honestly say that I had found true love. What I had been truly looking for was a spectacular and inevitable failure. I was to prove I was single through lack of other options. But since my first two dates I had begun to see possibilities of a successful conclusion. Still, it was good to hear a voice of experience telling me that, so long as I remained honest with everyone, I wouldn't be wasting anyone's time.

While I was reading Jeff's reply, an email arrived from my literary agent in which he told me that the film rights for *Marry Me* were under discussion with a hot LA agent. I switched the computer off and stared at it, uncertain whether to laugh or not. A movie!

A demon appeared in my head and I could almost see his demonic grin stretching. 'You need to date a lot of women,' he said.

'How many's a lot?' I asked.

'Jeff did seventy-eight. You should do at least seventy-nine.'

'I'm not in competition with Jeff.'

'You're looking for your ideal partner. Now, if you're going to take that seriously you need to meet a large number of women. And you have to beat Jeff.'

'I don't even know the guy, and anyway he's helping me. This isn't about numbers, it's about love.'

'Do you know how to find a carpet you love? Visit a shop with lots of carpet samples.'

'Women aren't carpets.'

'They used to be – that's bloody feminism for you. Let's say you meet seventy-seven women and you don't find your ideal partner. What will everyone say?'

'I hope they'll respect the effort I made.'

'They'll say that's the guy who dated fewer women than Jeff Cohen. This could be a movie. Do you want it to be a movie about you or Jeff Cohen?'

'But I might have already met my ideal partner. If Heather said she'd marry me tomorrow, I'd do it.'

'Then it'll be a crap film. You've got pathetically few girls to arrange more dates with. You have to start making things happen. No one wants to watch a movie about a man who goes out with only a handful of women. Brad Pitt won't want to play you.'

'Go away,' I said, and he did, and my brain filled again with candy-coated thoughts of love finding me in its own sweet way.

Soon afterwards, Heather wrote me a nice email explaining why she didn't want to continue seeing me. My rush-job, love-at-first-sight search for a wife was incompatible to her realistic getting-to-know-you, slow-burn idea of romance. She wanted to find something more stable and normal. This reason I understood, but it left me wondering if my search stood much of a chance when there were so many good and bad reasons to turn me away. I think Heather might have been too classically romantic for me anyway, but I was glad to have met her and hoped to meet her again as a friend. We did stay in contact.

MINI-DATES

I started announcing on stage at every gig that I was looking for a wife. On the very first occasion, a beautiful lady approached me at the bar. She had Scandinavian-blonde hair, firm, eye-magnet breasts, legs as graceful as brush strokes and swaying hips that continued to sway even when she stood still. I knew what her hips were trying to sway.

'I 'eard yer announcement and I fink yer should marry me,' she said in an East London accent. I was about to say, 'Yes,' when she continued, 'friend Elizabeth.'

I looked over at Elizabeth. She was occupying two chairs, leaning forward in a sumo-wrestler stance, wearing several pairs of spectacles – well, it may have just been one extremely thick pair – and she had a somewhat hirsute face. She flared her nostrils at me and snorted.

I broke my vow of honesty. 'The marriage thing was just a joke,' I said. 'It's part of my act.'

The blonde girl left the bar, her hips still swaying. I remembered that I'd never been good at hip-reading.

I developed a new policy for those who approached me at gigs. I would take the girl somewhere private like backstage, or to a quiet area of the bar, and we would have a short date, during which we could decide if we should have a proper going-out-somewhere date. Those short dates were still dates, I figured, because they were one-on-one quality time and because no one has ever made an official rule over how much time constitutes a date.

Of the girls who were most notable on these mini-dates, there was a Jennifer who had travelled to every single country I could name, a Mandy who was a weightlifter and the most muscle-bound woman I have ever been so close to, a Janet who had such an outrageous laugh that I had to take her out of the club and go and get a drink next door because she was ruining the show, a Marie who was fascinating to talk to about music, and a designer called Fiona who was wearing a quite impressive and unusual suit that she had made herself. They were not all good; one girl looked and spoke as if she was breaking Earth's gravity.

March had brought me eight of these mini-dates. I didn't think any of them would make me a good bride, however, and I told them so as Jeff would have had me do. In Brighton, though, I met an exquisite Amy.

Amy

She was well pretty and pretty well out of my league. But a suit of bold takes the wearer up a league.

We spent half an hour together in the closed-off area of the bar while another act was on stage. 'So are you really looking for a wife or is that just material?' she asked.

'The experiment is to see if I can find my ideal partner, and if I do I shall marry her.' I congratulated myself on being honest this time.

'What if she doesn't want to marry you?'

'She has to. It's a rule.' I bought us both a drink. 'Would you be up for marrying me?'

'I wouldn't marry a man after just one drink,' she said. 'I'm not easy.'

I bought her another two drinks immediately. 'Now will you marry me?'

'OK.'

We long-slow-kissed goodbye and drew slowly apart. Then her eyelids fluttered over her misty eyes and she moved to kiss me goodbye again. We said goodbye to each other many times. Whoever said goodbyes are hard has not said goodbye to Amy.

I left Brighton with Amy's number and a tingly feeling tapping 'Maybe' in Morse code down my spine.

My diary was too packed with gigs to arrange a date with her in the immediate future and I already had three dates arranged on my coming days off. To cancel those dates in the belief that I had found my wife would be a bit rash. If I was meant to be with Amy, she would wait a couple of weeks.

End-of-March Report

I'd been on eleven dates. I'd lost two potential wives (Heather and Rosie). The potential wives who remained were Becky the Uncontactable, Amy the Spinetingler, Loki the God of Mischief, Jode of Prague, Meganetta the Giant, Sarah the Engaged, and Paige the American.

The mood was complex. My feelings fluctuated between romantic and cheap. I felt romantic about Heather but on losing her I immediately met Amy and felt all romantic again. I could not lose sight of my mission though, and Jeff Cohen had validated my ideas of what it meant to go on a wife-hunt.

I hadn't yet started on the list of things that would make me eligible but I'd *definitely* get down to it in April.

APRIL:
GIRLS AND GIGGLES

Loki: Second Date

My second date with Loki was as much fun as the first. I left her home with an agreement that we would meet again soon but I also had the feeling that she just wanted some fun and nothing more. I didn't know what I wanted. I thought she was great and wonderful company, but I hadn't yet established what I was looking for in a wife.

Susie

She had a round, red-pink face that was like looking into a tub of strawberry ice-cream. She was fat, stinky and her hair was a mess of knots which were more complex than anything a sailor could tie.

We met in a comedy club because of my mission announcement on stage. Over by the bar we got on brilliantly by insulting each other. I told her I'd get the final insult in when I described her in my book. She told me that she would write a book called *Carey Marx is Stupid and Ugly*. We arranged a proper going-out date in London.

In a pub in Leicester Square, Susie demonstrated her ability to write backwards rapidly. I challenged her with increasingly difficult sentences. She achieved them all so I told her I was unimpressed. I showed her a magic trick in which she gave me a two-pound coin from her handbag. I stroked the coin gently until it split in two and the two halves fell to the table and became one-pound coins. She gulped surprise and then immediately composed herself and described the trick as 'shit'. We spent a couple of hours playing slot-machine games. She celebrated heartily after beating me at a motor-car rally. I didn't feel like much of a loser because I'd beaten her eight times before her win.

She told me she was taking a course to become a bus driver. I'm not looking to marry a bus driver.

Susie and I will no doubt meet again because we developed such a good relationship, based on antagonising each other. But though I loved spending time with her I wasn't in love with her. If I'd been in love with her, I could have still married her despite her decision to become a bus driver. It isn't that she wanted to be a bus driver so much as that she didn't want to be anything, so driving buses would do. I'm not prejudiced against bus drivers, but my ideal wife would have greater ambition than Susie had. That doesn't mean my ideal wife won't turn out to be a bus driver, but being a bus driver isn't on the Desired Characteristics list. If this sounds supercilious, consider how odd it would sound if I declared that my ideal wife *would* be a bus driver. I don't want to marry a man, either, but I've no animosity towards men.

When I told someone I didn't want to marry Susie because she was unambitious, I was accused of being insulting. But it isn't an insult to state a personal preference in romantic partners. It's simply mature and honest.

Lesson

I do not have to marry a bus driver if I do not want to.

Vicki

She found me on one of the dating sites I'd joined, and wrote to me in early March.

> So is everything a joke to you? Sorry, crap question. I love and loathe this site at the same time. Good luck with wife finding, I'll look out for your book next year.

I wrote back:

> As far as your sceptical thoughts on this site – me too. That's something I want to cover in the book. But did you write to me to tell me that you don't fully trust this web-dating thing, or to wish me good luck finding a wife, or just to ask if everything is a joke to me … ? Or did you contact me to say, 'Hi, let's chat'? If so, you forgot to mention that bit.
>
> Sure, you might love and loathe this site but just think, on it you might find someone you can love and loathe.

She wrote:

> Mainly curious to see if everything is a joke to you (which I didn't mean in a nasty way, although writing this now I realise that's how it might have come across, sorry). Thank you for raising some very good points and now I have your attention are you replying just out

of politeness or because you'd like to chat? See that's my problem, I've just read that last sentence and I'd like to chat but there are a thousand things that when I write them down can appear to come across wrong and I know what I mean but it's all down to your interpretation. Putting my brain into gear before I put my mouth into action is much easier verbally than (orally?) on e-mail and I'm sure it should be the other way round. Now my boss wants his computer back so I'll have to go. Phew saved by the boss that doesn't happen often.

Two days later she wrote again, and she commented in her email that I looked more relaxed in one of the new pictures on my profile.

Uncertain what to make of Vicki, I asked which picture I didn't look relaxed in, accused her of coming across in her emails as either a bit dithery, dizzy and self-deprecating or else quirky and funny, and admitted that I couldn't decide which I thought she was.

She replied that she was only dithery on computer, that she'd never been called dizzy, but had been called quirky and funny. Self-deprecation, she assured me, is something she exhibits only once or twice a year; she was glad she'd got it out of the way for this year and she apologised that I had to witness it. She said that the photo I didn't look relaxed in was one in which I had my arms folded.

I replied:

You're wrong about me not being relaxed. I always cross my arms when I relax. I have my arms crossed now. It's making it difficult to type, but it's oh so relaxing.

Anyway, we seem to be getting on right well. You've told me that

I might not be relaxed. I've told you that you might be dizzy. We've both denied the charges. I think this is a good start.

So, will you marry me?

On 5 April I returned from some gigs and found two emails from Vicki. The second said:

Hi. Actually maybe we should get married, it feels like we'd be perfect. You're already ignoring me, we've done the name calling and we're not having sex, all that's missing really is the ceremony and certificate!

We met by the bagel stand in Waterloo station. As I reached her, a friend called Cogs rang my mobile. He offered a girl he had once dated. So, while on a date with one girl I was being offered another girl. I was having a pretty good time of life, I guess.

Vicki and I had a drink and went off looking for somewhere to eat. We passed the London Eye and considered taking a ride on it, but it had closed. We found a nice Chinese restaurant overlooking the Thames and the night-lit Houses of Parliament.

I like Chinese food. I made a decision to steer as many of my dates to Chinese restaurants as possible.

A redhead of about my height, Vicki works as a primary school teacher. It was a cool date with a lady who, despite the way she may have come across in her first emails, is relaxed, self-assured and very good company. She told me that I had been the best of her internet dates so far. I was the second. I told her to let me know how I fared after the third.

When I arrived home, Paige called from America. We spoke for an hour and a half. This time she was sober and a whole lot of fun. I was glad I hadn't wiped her off my list but I had no idea how we'd ever be able to meet.

Top of my list was still Amy, who had made my spine tingle and had made me think that I really could be up for marrying this year if we continued to get along well as we had the first time we met.

The Embarrassment Factor

By early April, I'd given up trying to contact Becky and found myself constantly on the phone, and constantly trying to find internet access on my travels in order to keep up with all the email writing. It often took a number of emails before a date was at last fixed up.

Many of the women were put off by the book and show associated with my mission. A girl called Sam, with whom I'd exchanged over a dozen emails, wrote:

> I have been thinking about this and decided that I do not want my private life publicly documented even in pseudonym form. Sorry. I wish you all the best with your search for a wife and will come and see the show in Edinburgh and read the book when it comes out. It's been fun talking.

I had a number of similar disappointments, including Danielle, the girl who'd asked for a washing machine instead of a bicycle.

Dating sites had first seemed to me a relaxed, friendly way to meet people. I'd heard a few criticisms that made little sense. One woman told me she thought they were an unnatural way to meet people. But most things these days are unnatural. We commute to work, use mobile phones and watch television. Dating sites meet a need that's right at the heart of our modern age. It's surely sagacious to try as many methods as possible of finding something you want. If you join a dating site it doesn't mean you can't also meet someone in a nightclub.

However, I found that most of the women on the sites disagreed. It turns out that dating is considered private and an almost taboo subject for many ladies. I can see the reasons for this, but I don't think they're good reasons. Quite a few women told me that even their friends didn't know they were using the sites.

Reality shows on television give the false impression that the public loves any opportunity to appear in the media. We tend to forget that we're seeing only the extrovert attention-seekers. I relate more to people who aren't that extrovert, and yet I couldn't relate to the many people I came across who were scared of what other people might think of them for merely going out on a date.

I might as well have been investigating a drugs ring, and certainly felt as if I was deeply involved in a covert operation. I'd been so uninformed when I took on the mission. I'd expected that nobody would mind going out on a fun date with a comedian and being part of a semi-comical and harmless search for a wife.

Lesson

I wasn't looking for a super-confident woman, but I didn't want one who found being herself embarrassing. I didn't want a woman who would come running to me solely because of my show and book, neither did I want a woman who was afraid of them.

My wife wouldn't be the type to be embarrassed about going out dating while being free and single. I wanted a woman who was too cool for such timorousness.

Although I made it absolutely clear that I was writing a show and a book, many ladies entered into written communication with me and kept that communication going for quite a while before changing their minds. I realised that I would have to play a huge game of numbers to find the kind of cool ladies I was looking for.

During this time, I'd become extremely busy with work. I gigged all over the country, spending most of my time travelling, and I had a mountain of work to do for the Edinburgh Festival. I urgently needed a photo session for the Festival brochure, and equally urgently needed to sign contracts, fill in forms, take on management, book a venue and so on. I cancelled some gigs at a ski resort in France.

I rang Amy to confirm a date I'd put in the diary with her, and to see if I could move it forward to the week I'd just freed. She told me she'd just met and started seeing someone else. She apologised and said that she hadn't thought I was particularly interested in her because I hadn't contacted her often since our meeting.

I explained that I'd been busy and that I'd been excited about our next date. I'd phoned her once but she was out and there was no answering machine. She told me her phone didn't always work properly. She said again that she'd begun to believe I wasn't interested. And she told me that the man she'd started seeing was an ex, and then she cried during a confession of feeling confused. Remembering my vow that, whether it ended in success or failure, I'd get through my mission without hurting anyone, I told her to investigate her new romance but if it went belly up to contact me again. We laughed about it.

I shrugged a lot for the rest of that evening.

Lesson

I could not afford to let this mistake happen again. If I met a girl who showed great potential, I'd devote enough time to her to make it clear that I fancied her, and would see if we could see each other intensely for a short time to find out where our relationship might be going. On the other hand, because of my mission I couldn't afford to get stuck in a relationship which blew all the others out and then went nowhere fast. Apart from anything else, if I put all my eggs in one basket and the basket didn't want to marry me, I wouldn't have a show. Still, I wouldn't let another Amy incident happen.

GOOD TIMES

I had two gigs a night over the weekend in London so I squeezed in a few dates before, between and after. One was with a Louise, who wrote to me after seeing my act in a comedy club.

She was lovely, amusing and smart. But she was also eighteen and had an eighteen-year-old's life that I had nothing in common with at all. On the other hand, she could out-drink a thirty-nine-year-old man quite easily. I went on to my gig drunk.

Between gigs I met a girl called Helen, who was also very young. She'd seen me performing in Croydon in March and written to my website. I found her winsome and funny, but we agreed that our compatibility rating was low. I suggested it was our age difference. She disagreed and then talked for some time about bands I'd never heard of.

On the Saturday, I hooked up with a thirty-two-year-old woman called Terry, whose friend had taken my number when I was in Glasgow in February. Terry's flame-yellow hair looked like a bonfire. She had a most captivating face, and I told her so because she deserved to know. Her eye colour seemed to switch between green and blue as her expressions altered. I was fascinated. I took her for a Chinese meal. We discussed dating, and she told me she'd been taken out on a date only four times in her life. I said people should be less embarrassed about dating. She agreed, and we had a fun meal, perhaps helped by her agreement, because I always find that such behaviour helps people get along well with me.

'Perhaps you don't need to go on dates,' I told her. 'You seem very gregarious. I expect you just meet people naturally.'

This time she disagreed. She didn't like dating men from her workplace because of political complications, and most of her friends were married or in relationships. But she told me she was enjoying our date and it had made her decide to start dating more often.

'So you're not enjoying the date enough to marry me?' I asked.

She put her hand on mine. 'No, I don't think I'm going to marry you, but I do like you and want to see you again. You've made me realise that dating's fun and I should join one of those agencies you told me about.'

'In other words, I've impressed you so much that you want to see other men.'

'You should take it as a compliment.'

Lesson

I didn't want to become a dating guru, but I was enjoying dating and could put out a positive message. Everybody I met wanted to talk to me about what I was up to, and many people seemed affected by my view of dating. In America dating's far more acceptable and normal. In Britain people are as reserved on the subject as they are about most things. Even if I didn't find a wife this way, I'd discovered the dating scene and found that other people were gaining from my experience.

Secrets of
Internet Dating

An American site on the internet gives advice on writing the perfect profile to attract the ladies. The site's expert teaches his system to get the girlies. He has the usual acronym-based rule system that all self-help advisers have, and he breaks down an ordinary advert to show what's wrong with it. He advises that the advert must capture the girl's imagination, draw her in, present her with a challenge and give her a feeling of inclusion in something special. He offers an analogy involving a car salesman he met. Then he gives us his perfect dating-ad. The heading asks: 'ARE YOU PREPARED TO TAKE THE $60 CHALLENGE?'

This, of course, will make the girl go gooey. 'The $60 challenge! Why, of course. What is it? I must know. I must take it. Please!'

He follows his attention-grabbing heading with a painfully salesman-like advert, including the use of repetition and the suggestion that she 'cannot believe it'. He offers to prove that he can take the girl to a five-star restaurant and get a meal for just $30 each. Yes, just $30 each. He finishes by asking if she will be his cohort on this exciting date. What a nut. It would be good, though, if the girl turned up and discovered that he'd used the word 'cohort' in its proper sense and expected her to dress as an ancient Roman military unit.

The dating sites had been great entertainment.

On the downside, many of them run cons such as a free trial membership which finishes as soon as you've finished filling in all the forms. Some go on sending you emails after you have said you aren't interested, and it can be hard to get rid of them. I'm not recommending any particular site, because I have at least one complaint about each one that I used. I'm only recommending the concept. To the sites, I would suggest the following rules if you want people like me to put in a word for you:

1   Offer a genuinely free trial membership.

2   Offer a person rather than a company name for people to deal directly with. Many people are embarrassed about joining these sites and humans require human encouragement. One company I wrote to responded with an email signed by their company. I complained about the impersonal response, and asked if I could talk to a human. The reply came instantly. It was an automated response telling me my complaint number (135724).

3   Drop all strong-arm tactics such as those used by one site which constantly emails me telling me that unless I pay up I won't find out about the two beautiful women who are trying to contact me.

4   Sort out your technical problems. Many of the sites lost emails I sent, or claimed that I'd received emails which didn't show in the site's inbox.

I've become a staunch supporter and defender of these sites, though they seem to vary hugely in effectiveness. There's one site from which I neither managed to gain a single date nor had a reply from anyone remotely interesting.

Because of the stigma attached to these sites, many people don't tell anyone that they're using this method of meeting people. I'm trying to spread the word that they should all relax. Upping your chances of finding something you want is logically an intelligent choice which should make you feel shrewd and buoyant, not ashamed. Join a site and then leap up and down in the street shouting about how clever you are. Then you'll have something to feel ashamed about.

It's hard to say something different in your profile, but do it anyway. Not all of us are geniuses but it is actually quite easy to avoid being hack at anything. Simply figure out what a hack would do and don't do it. Scroll through some of the other profiles and you'll soon get to know the clichés such as 'I like to have fun'. I assume most people like to have fun, unless they tell me otherwise. At all costs avoid 'I'm bubbly' unless you're on a website for teenage girls looking for other teenage girls. Bubbles are empty. Some old ladies' legs are bubbly. Just stop being bubbly.

Don't go on about things you don't like in people. You may think you're weeding out the undesirables, but in fact you're being one. Say what things you do like. You'll attract people with these traits, and they'll immediately feel a connection with you because they'll feel appreciated for having those traits. For instance, instead of writing 'I don't want anyone messy' write 'I particularly like tidy people'. You'll probably get a rush of mail from anal retentives, and you deserve them. The point is: talk positive and don't paint a picture of yourself as a whiner. No one likes whiners, and that includes you – even if you are one. Whiners whine about everything, including other whiners.

If you're a lousy speller, write your profile in a word-processing programme which has a spell-checker, and then cut and paste it into your profile. Do the same with every 'flirt' (or local word used by the site) you send. It may seem a little dishonest, but it's no different from asking a friend's advice about what to wear for a date. I'm not bothered about the occasional misspelling or malapropism – I'm certainly capable of both – but some of the emails I received were so riddled with careless errors that I was put off the writer.

Finally, don't get addicted. I've only behaved like a dating-site addict, but I've met a few real ones. The sites are accessories to your single life. People work hard on their careers and yet they expect their private life to sort itself out without effort. Don't plant a brick and wait for a house to grow. Build it yourself.

MIA

I met Mia on an internet dating site. In her profile she said, 'I am a very intense, humourless harridan lacking in most social graces and all common sense. I would like someone butterscotch flavoured. Please.' She also said she'd like to find someone within a five-mile radius.

I wrote:

I think it's a bit ambitious of you to be looking for someone butterscotch-flavoured within a five-mile radius. Ten miles, perhaps. I am not the man for you because I am not butterscotch-flavoured, so really I am just writing with this ten-mile radius advice, which I hope was of some help. On the other hand, I can be rum-raisin flavoured on a warm afternoon and spend most of my time being more banana and peach (though I have to admit to getting a bit stale-tomato between the hours of 9pm and 10pm; we can't all be perfect).

Anyway, despite being the wrong flavour for your taste, I work as a comedian and have had enough of laughter and fun, so your promise of a lack of humour is very inviting to me. Mixing with you might help me wind down after a gig.

A few days later, she replied.

> Your thoughtful advice warmed my spleen and made me reconsider the parameters of my flavouring requirements. I will expand my catchment area to 10 miles and pray that I do not receive an influx of aubergine-tasting date prospects.
>
> I would like to meet you but think it only fair to confess up front that I come with baggage of the sort that cannot easily be checked into a locker room for a few hours or left to circle endlessly around a carousel. And don't think I haven't tried. Also, my mother is no longer Irish, although she can still be plied with gin nonetheless.
>
> Moreover, I cannot marry you and accept the offer of a bicycle wedding gift, much as I would like for our love to unfold in this way (and then refold again like a Brompton). The reason being? You are a Canadian and I swore long ago, never to get involved with another Canadian (strange though that you think it a profession and not a nationality).
>
> Regrettably, we can never be. It is possible, however, that we might be fiends and enjoy a mutually rewarding fiendship in which together we battle against the evil forces of funny things, fun times and fungus.
>
> Be warned. I AM a harridan. You may call me Harry for short.

I wrote back saying that she deserved to get dates who tasted of dates and that I thought it would be good to start a fiendship with her. I guessed that the baggage she referred to was a child and assured her that she was wrong about not being able to leave him or her in a locker room or on a carousel. She was also wrong that I am Canadian, so she could, indeed, marry me.

She replied agreeing to a date, though saying she was a little cautious. She complained that my photos showed me as too good-looking. She also explained that Canadian was a mishearing of comedian. I replied that she should get the voice in her head to repeat things, that the photos were taken by a friend who's a very good photographer, and that in real life I have green skin and eyes that can see 360 degrees. I have never tried to attract a girl before by assuring her that I'm not handsome.

I invited Mia to a gig and spotted her in the audience right away, even though she was not disguised as a cheese-grater, which she said she would be. Liar. She is mixed-race, attractive, a scientist/researcher and has a very odd, slightly sarcastic, self-deprecating sense of humour. After the gig, I sat with Mia and her friend while Adrian, who runs the gig, cleared away the audience and all the other tables and then came over a few times to bring us drinks – what a gentleman.

Mia asked how my mission was going and I told her about my recent dates. She told me that I had things a bit good and I agreed, because I had. Her sense of humour allows her to talk with some obfuscation and I was never quite sure whether Mia was after a relationship, marriage, or just some fun. I asked a few times but none of the asking brought a direct answer. She did seem fun, funny and interesting, and I told her I'd like to see her again. It was too soon to say if she would be wife potential.

I did not know the next date was going to be a date.

On the first weekend in April, in London's Comedy Store an extremely beautiful young Italian girl passed me while I was heading to the bar. To call her fit would be an insult to just how fit she was. If you could lower your eyes from her stunning face you were in for even more treats, each of them sparsely wrapped.

Later, she passed me again and said she'd enjoyed my act. She was

working on a student project to do with romance, and asked if I'd
agree to an interview. I gave her my number.

Selina (aka the spanner in the works)

I arrived at a pub in Leicester Square for the interview. She drank
wine. I drank cola and told her I didn't have long because I was busy
finding a wife. I told her about the recent goings-on with my mission.

'Am I one of your possible wives?' she asked.

I gave what I thought was the right answer, 'No. You're a student
conducting an interview.'

'I'd be happy to be one of your dates.' Her smile beamed through
my eyes and straight down to my groin. I thought it a bit strange
because she was twenty-one and dazzling, but, well, if she wanted to
be one of my potential wives, I mean, that was her decision. She
decided that she did and said she hoped at least to make the third
phase of selection. I knew that would be easy because she'd be
impossible for me to deselect. It became a date and I fetched us both
some wine.

She conducted her interview about romance being something
many people have no time for. We somehow started talking about sex
and we talked candidly. Selina turned out to be an exhibitionist and a
lot into anything else you can think of. I was fascinated. I showed her
my camera and asked if I could get a picture of her. I took a picture. I
took some more. We went to the park with some strawberries and
champagne. I took more pictures. I arrived home shaking my head in
disbelief that we hadn't been arrested: we'd broken several laws to do
with indecent behaviour in public.

A few moments after I arrived home, Christian, my Edinburgh
promoter, rang to discuss how well my show was coming together. He
told me that he was worried about me going on lots of dates and

therefore drinking a lot and not getting the show written. I assured
him that I'd achieved a lot that day.

Lesson

I wouldn't marry Selina, though if she asked me I would.
Her soul is too freelance to offer a contract to. I agreed to see
her again, even though there was no chance of us marrying,
because I couldn't say and mean no when she asked if we
could see each other again. I've never got on that well with
prudes. I do get on well with women who are open-minded,
imaginative and daring. Women seem to be capable of vast
leaps in fantasyland which can seem perverted when coming
from a man. My wife might not be Selina, but she would
have a sense of adventure and a relaxed attitude to carnal
fun.

EMILY

She turned up for our date in a West End London pub wearing a regimental-blue silk blouse and a mud-brown denim skirt. I told her I was surprised that her colour scheme worked to such harmonious effect. Delighted, she told me that her friends had said much the same thing. We'd got off to a good start, and I mentally congratulated myself because I was learning to talk girl.

Emily had been given my number by Terry, whom I had dated three days earlier. I took her for a Chinese meal and we got on splendidly.

'I think it's hilarious that my dates are now setting me up with other dates,' I told her.

'Terry said she wasn't going to marry you but she thought I might.'

'Do you think you might?'

'I might. I think we should go on somewhere and discuss it.'

We'd downed a fair bit of alcohol and going on somewhere to discuss anything seemed sensible.

At a table nearby, another couple were clearly on a date. His fluffy moustache had kindly saved his mouth from devouring too much sweet-and-sour sauce. The woman's stiff, thorny posture and the man's fidgety tapping on the table were such explicit body-language signs that a goldfish could have told that the couple were distressed. I looked at my date, relaxed and comfortable under her dark-haired fringe, her face boasting youthful eyes and frisky lips whose every kiss would be mesmerising. I thought steam would fizz from my skin as her finger slid down my naked arm. I fancied her.

'C'mon, let's go on somewhere and have some fun,' she said.

'I'm not supposed to be having fun,' I told her, thinking about Christian's warning. 'I'm supposed to be finding a wife.'

'That sounds like it should be fun,' she said. 'How are you going to know if someone's the right wife if you don't have fun with her?'

'I don't know. It's a quandary.' I made a mental note to put the question to Christian.

The woman on the table nearby asked for the bill as soon as her date had finished his last bite. She wanted home. She left before he did. Emily asked for our bill a moment later. She wanted fun. We left together.

Lesson

Emily is extremely attractive. Her best trait is a natural conviviality. I felt comfortable talking, laughing and joking about any subject with her. Her ease with and amusement at my mission were extensions of this trait. I realised that it would be part of being ideal for my ideal partner to have this characteristic and the best way to ensure that would be to marry Emily. She said, 'One step at a time.' She said, 'We'll meet again soon.' She said, 'Who knows what will happen?'

Everything was going so swimmingly that I'd relinquished my meaningful proof-that-romance-is-over-idolised failure plan, because success seemed to be wearing a saddle with easy-climb stirrups attached. Maybe things wouldn't work out with Emily, but I'd certainly keep in contact with her and prevent another Amy-mishap. Whether it worked out or not, I was meeting fabulous women and loving the dating. All the girls were happy. All the girls were worth my time. I had discovered romance and it was loaded with unexpected wonders.

The lascivious interest of the dusky-skinned Selina had taken me totally by surprise, like coming across Attila the Hun in heaven. She left my ego opulent. And then Emily had stirred in me an ebullient enthusiasm for my mission.

Friends were all taking an interest. Friends of friends were taking an interest. Friends of friends of friends were taking an interest. Regularly, I was informed that I was a genius. Soon the whole world would know about my simple mission – my experiment in the elusive or candid nature of love. So far, I had good news for everybody and everybody loved to hear it.

One friend of a friend of a friend was unimpressed, and with a jaundiced slant on my mission he said, 'I still don't think you'll manage to find a wife by the end of the Edinburgh Festival, though. I reckon you'll come out of it a failure. You're bound to lose.'

I corrected him swiftly because understanding my mission statement was vital. 'I'm seeing if it's possible to find my ideal bride *this year*. Finding her by the end of August was just the original gimmick-idea, which I dropped. I can't lose. It isn't a bet. Think of this as a scientist testing the effect of a drug. The test itself may succeed or fail, but so long as the scientist proves the drug works or does not work he's carried out the test successfully. Whatever the outcome of the test, the scientist is only a failure if he hasn't performed his experiment diligently.'

This position had become important to me. I wanted the freedom to fail, rather than have to force an outcome for cheap gratification. I was glad of the chance to raise the issue and express myself clearly.

'I still think you'll lose and come out of it a failure,' he said.

I had no idea how it would all end. I knew only that I was giddy with my new lifestyle and new female friends.

While I was walking through central London at around midnight, my phone beeped. I had a text message from Selina, asking if I wanted to come round and see her. A few moments later, I had a text from a girl I'd had a mini-date with at a comedy club, back in March; she asked what I was up to. Another text appeared moments later from Emily. Another two girls I had met recently because of my wife-search sent me text messages. This was not totally surprising. By now I was spending much of my time on the phone and receiving constant text messages, but receiving five such invitations within the space of a few minutes woke me up to a realisation. As I walked along Oxford Street staring at my phone, it dawned on me for the first time that everybody else was right: I am a genius.

Still staring at my phone, I walked into a lamppost.

I called Jode in Prague and she sounded so good that I immediately booked a flight for the beginning of June. Karen, a girl who was booking me for a gig in Phoenix, rang to say that I should date her friend Emma, whom she described as beautiful. She passed the phone over and I arranged to meet Emma in London on the coming Wednesday after she finished work.

CYCLOPS AND THE ZOMBIES

I discovered a girl whose nickname was the name of a mythical monster, and here our story starts to slip into a quagmire of moral complication. We shall know her as Cyclops; this name is an apt slant on the nickname she used on the website.

She had something to say about herself. She answered all the profile questions with solid, imaginative, and sometimes cutting remarks. My interest was aroused and I took an instant liking to her. She came across as unusual and intriguing. She described herself as a hardcore atheist, CND supporter, left-wing, pacifist, feminist, non-drug-taking, vegetarian, existentialist who was nearly a tree-hugger. That is a lot of things to be. I was not any of them, but I wanted to meet someone with so much attitude, especially if she had a sense of humour to go with it. I wrote to her,

> Cyclops
>
> I have read your profile and reached the conclusion that I could change you into my perfect wife. It will take a bit of effort, I think,

and I hope that you recognise the compliment that I am considering going to all that effort on our behalf.

First of all, I will change you from a hardcore atheist to an atheist. You are 34 and that is too old to be hardcore about not believing in nothing. I do not believe that there is an invisible book on my head right now, and inflating that belief is giving too much credence to anyone who suggests that there is an invisible book on my head right now. A 34-year-old wife, as you soon shall be (unless it's your birthday soon), should offer such a person a smile of pity and simply say, gently, 'No there isn't an invisible book on my head right now.' It would be unbecoming of her to be all hardcore about it, perhaps thumping her head, doing headstands, using a torch to demonstrate light passing uninterrupted above her head and whatever else one of you hardcore types would do in this situation.

Secondly, while I will let you keep your tree-not-far-off-from-hugging left-wing views, and will let you display these tendencies and views around friends of mine who will find it all cute, there will be times that I will expect you to nod, smile and remain silent, especially around my tree-felling hobbyist friends. We stand round trees and shout, 'Furniture plants!' at them.

Thirdly, you will learn to make a nuclear bomb, and will go to war with me if there is any threat to our great Nation.

Fourthly, you will be allowed to use the word 'existential' only once a day.

Fifthly, you must learn how to butcher meat and do it the kosher way how God would like it. Or rather how He would like us to have it.

Sixthly, you will reconsider your view of drugs. It is best to do this while on drugs.

Finally, you will pay for the meal at our first date as a gesture to show that you have your feminist problem under control and that it won't become an issue. If you don't do this I will consider you anti-Semitic.

I think that with effort on both our parts we can implement these changes in time for our wedding, which I have booked. Oh, and that's the other thing: you will have to buy into the idea of marriage, which I am guessing you presently have no respect for. I enjoyed your profile very much and think that I could easily fall in love with what you will become.

Carey

I received a reply saying she couldn't marry me because she'd read my profile and realised I was not after her but rather after any desperately shelved woman who'd marry me in a hurry. She also said that she could never go anywhere near meat. But she did at least admit that she'd found my email funny and she signed with her real name, which I thought was enough of a reason to write back.

I explained the concept of the show, how I was mostly speaking to very nice women and how the project had changed. I added:

I am disgusted that you have made me write you a serious response. You feminists.

I think the meat issue might have been a biggie anyway. I eat it. You are so hardline. By the way, I'm not attracting or after desperately-shelved women. I wrote to you because you seemed non-desperately-shelved. And very funny. OK, I've tried being funny with you and now I'm trying being serious with you. Next, I will try being semi-serious. Then I will try existentially nonplussed. What if I only eat meat when you aren't looking? This would be out of respect rather than dishonesty. Or I'll wrap it in cabbage. Godammit, you're hard to please. What if I become a vegetable? Then will you love me?

In her reply she made some suggestions for my show, including some marriage get-out clauses, and asked how to pronounce my name correctly. I responded:

> Delighted that you wrote back, which was the right decision. Well done. Good girl. For that, you don't deserve in any way to be patronised. Sorry. But I am proud of you doing the right thing. You get a gold star.

I told her how to pronounce my name (as in the word 'care', with an 'ee' sound at the end; it should sound as if you're describing me as someone who cares). And I said:

> Your back-up plans for my project are viable, and I have considered many other get-out clauses. But they ruin the fun. I'm flying without a harness on this one. Trapezing without a safety net. Playing cricket without shin-pads. Listening to Leonard Cohen on ecstasy. Driving without due care and attention. Playing cards with elderly amputees. Making Lego houses with real bricks instead of Lego. Using metaphors that don't mean anything. Somewhere out there might be the girl I will spend the rest of my life with. I don't know and don't believe that she's there; but I don't know and don't believe that she's not. I'm going to do my darndest to find out. I'm on a search. I'm prepared to pull out all the stops and even to use the word 'darndest'.

She wrote back saying that she'd be willing to be involved in my mission so long as I employed a pseudonym for her in my show because of her job — she didn't want her clients to hear about her private life on the single scene. And she asked where I'd be taking her on our date. I replied:

Honolulu.

Actually, that's the second date. How about a bicycle ride along the Thames or a trip to Birmingham or a coffee in a local bookshop or a West End musical or the circus or some left-wing talk about something somewhere or a stroll through Hyde Park on a warm afternoon or a swimming lesson or a museum or to the Globe or to a house party or a weather station or a book club or a day in Paris or an indoor ski slope or a riverboat or an acoustic music night or a dream factory whatever that is or bingo or shopping for a new T-shirt. I have lots of other suggestions.

An ominous reply arrived a couple of days later. She said she'd leave the date up to me, but then went on to request a date which involved danger! She claimed that a feeling of exhilaration would later be connected with the person you were with when you felt it.

I announced to my friends that my existentialist possible-wife wanted a surprise dangerous date and that I wanted to try and impress her with something tailor-made. We talked about scary dates.

My first ever date was with a girl in Christchurch, near Bournemouth. I was seventeen; she was about the same. I took her for a late-night walk along the River Stour, and into the graveyard. I used to enjoy a walk through the cemetery in Christchurch at night. It has a stonewall ruin and green lights that bathe the gravestones in spookiness, conjuring shadows and summoning phantoms in the imagination. I never got spooked, just seduced by the still serenity and isolation that clutched as you entered the place and gracefully detached itself as you stepped back out onto the white-lit street.

I had my first sexual experience with my date on a gravestone. I think it was her first, too. I didn't ask. I didn't know you could. I was so innocent. I knew some, but I'd heard rumours of so much more. The rumours conflicted, terrified and teased. I thought she loved it because of all the panting – panting's good, right? They're supposed to pant – the more noise the better – but they aren't supposed to foam at the mouth, are they? She was having an epileptic fit. My naivety at seventeen erupted with panicked interpretations. I wondered whether mouth-foam normally happens to a girl after sex. I'd heard that the female's orgasm was bigger than the male's but I hadn't expected it to explode out of every orifice in her body. I also had the horrifying thought that my orgasm had been far too powerful.

She was OK.

My friends and I devised the following date for my existentialist possible-wife: I'd take her to a graveyard at night for a picnic on the coming Sunday, which would be a full moon. Eva would make the picnic, which would include apt items such as a green frothing salad and eggs that looked like eyeballs. During the picnic, noises would be heard all around us, and then Michael Jackson's *Thriller* music would boom out and all my friends shuffle forward from behind gravestones dressed as zombies doing the *Thriller* dance from the video.

It would be a great date.

I also hoped Cyclops would turn out to be for real in everything she said, and not just someone who'd like to think she was extreme and unusual, having asked a stranger for a mystery date that involved danger. I gave her the benefit of the doubt, and took it that she did mean the words in her profile. It was also important that she meant it all with an element of humour, and her emails suggested she did. I adored the thought of meeting a truly unusual girl, but I didn't want to mess with someone who was insane or into mumbo-jumbo. There are a lot of thin lines to suss out with such promising women, and nutters often pass under my scanner as interesting and different during initial contact. They use being interesting as camouflage and don't display their nuttiness until they're ready to explode with it, for the same reason that bombs don't come in pretty colours.

Everyone agreed that they wanted to meet Cyclops, and we all hoped she'd love the date. I wrote to her:

Can you do this Sunday? Late evening.
> For this date I will need to know that you are definitely free and that you will definitely not back out.
> Once you have committed, there will be no going back.
> I think you will enjoy it.

She told me it sounded great and asked only for more detail about where we should meet.

The very gothic Highgate cemetery would be perfect, but it would be closed at night. I needed to find an open cemetery by Sunday.

While I was in Wales, I rang a London friend who lives in Stoke Newington, and he told me that his local cemetery stayed open at night. I sent a text to Cyclops to say that we'd meet there at nine o'clock on Sunday evening.

On Saturday evening, I returned from a gig in Loughborough to an all-night party.

6 a.m. Paul, who'd become my stunt-coordinator for the date, called a meeting in the back garden. We had a mammoth organisational task ahead of us if we were to bring off this masterpiece-date in the time. We needed a graveyard, zombies, *Thriller* music, something to play the music on, the picnic, night-vision cameras, masks . . . The idea was that Cyclops and I would wear masks to enhance the eerie atmosphere and then afterwards, if she found it all funny, she might let me use the video in my show because she'd be anonymous.

'There's only one thing we can be certain about,' said Paul with the calm authority of someone who knows exactly what he's doing. 'This date is going to be a shambles.'

We all drank to that because we were drunk enough to believe that a shambles was a good thing. Paul had made it sound good. He's Irish. They can do that.

A friend called Glenn offered to stand outside the cemetery as we arrived and say, 'I wouldn't go in there. I hear strange things happen in there.' At this point, housemate Nick opened one eye and added, 'Yes, I hear it's built on the site of an ancient burial ground.' Fun, fun, fun. We were having fun and couldn't conceive of a result that wouldn't be fun. It didn't have to come off perfectly. If it made Cyclops laugh, we'd declare it successful.

11 a.m. Matt had been glued to his phone all morning, ordering stuff and pleading with people for help with the date. He had several different plans for gaining an extra camera. Each of these plans involved other complications. Eva was still at the party and we couldn't get confirmation of whether the picnic had been made, but we were a little suspicious that it hadn't. Zombies were dropping out because the party had driven a stake's worth of party-juice into their hearts or because they had last minute-gigs to go to.

When I entered the lounge, Matt was staring at his phone and holding his head. 'I can't make another call,' he said.

'You have to,' said Paul, calm as ever.

Matt nodded bravely and made the call. He also called his parents to apologise that he could not come round for the family Passover meal because something more important had come up. Later, he rang home again to ask if he could borrow his father's camera.

5 p.m. Nick and Eva returned from the party so they could be zombies for the night. They came into the lounge and instantly fell so deeply asleep that they couldn't be woken. We had no choice but to take photos of them sleeping with a rubber severed hand (which one of the zombies would later be using) holding different parts of their anatomies. By now, we were fairly certain that Eva would not be creating an amazing picnic for the date.

Matt rang a friend of his called Richard to tell him that he had to be a zombie. There was a hitch: Richard was also supposed to be going to the Passover meal at Matt's family's home.

6 p.m. I received a call from my contact near the graveyard. He told me that he'd walked past it to double-check that it was open. He reported that it was locked and that he didn't know a way in. The walls would be difficult to climb, and anyway I couldn't imagine Cyclops agreeing to climb walls. We racked what was left of our brains and made more calls to see if we could find another cemetery. We drew blanks.

'We have to postpone this date,' said Paul.

'We can't,' I told him. 'I don't have another free day in my diary for a month and we won't be able to guarantee a full moon. I'll probably lose the girl. I don't want another Amy situation on my hands.'

Twenty minutes of bad news on other cemeteries arrived through mobile phones.

'Max,' said Paul. 'Ring Max. If anyone knows a graveyard that will be open, he will.'

Aah, Max. He loves a good walk and he loves to investigate. If there were a cemetery we could get into at night within a few miles of our area he'd certainly know.

'Yes,' said Max, 'I know somewhere perfect. I took the kid in there for a walk one night a while ago.'

7 p.m. On the phone to his father again, Matt explained that Richard wouldn't be able to go to the Passover dinner because we needed him and asked if it would be OK for Richard to go round there, grab the camera, and then come round to us. He marched up and down the hall. 'I was wondering if I could also borrow Richard for the evening? It's Mum I'm worried about upsetting, really, because she's cooked for us . . . No, his parents are fine with it . . . I think it's mainly Mum – in fact it is Mum. Why's she upset about . . . Well, I can ask Richard to bring over the honey-mustard dressing . . .' He finished the call with a thumbs-up.

I sent a text to Cyclops to tell her that she was now to meet me at East Finchley station. She texted me back to say that she'd sussed where I'd be taking her, because I'd warned her to dress warmly. She thought I was taking her ice-skating. I gulped. She'd meant a different type of danger. Surely she couldn't seriously think we'd find somewhere to ice-skate at that time of the evening, or that such a date would be considered dangerous? It was too late now. I just hoped that she'd enjoy the mock-danger I'd planned.

8 p.m. We hadn't managed to find a music player that worked on batteries, so Paul came up with a new variation for the date: during the cemetery picnic, I'd show Cyclops a card trick. I'd force the Ace of Diamonds. She'd look at it and put it back in the pack. I'd try to find the card and fail. Zombies would climb out from behind gravestones, murmuring, 'Ace of Diamonds.' I'm pretty good with a pack of cards and used to work as a magician, so forcing a card would be easy.

8.15 p.m. In the taxi en route, we discussed breaking into the cemetery, dressing as zombies and scaring a girl. The driver slowed the cab and threw me a suspicious look. 'We're going on a date,' I told him. He accepted this and carried on driving.

There was a quick discussion on the illegality of what we were about to do. Matt pointed out that no cop would arrest a bunch of people dressed as zombies because the rest of the force would call him Buffy for the remainder of his career.

We dropped Matt at the pub/meeting point. Paul and I went to check out the cemetery. It was huge. Paul led the way, looking for a perfect spot. He wanted somewhere well away from the path so that a security guard wouldn't see us and remove us. I was worried that, if it was too remote, Cyclops might feel in real danger.

8.40 p.m. We had no more time to plan. As we traipsed out of the darkening cemetery my enthusiasm for the date sobered to thoughts of a foreboding outcome. I was about to take a stranger in here. Maybe it would not be funny.

In the pub, the two cameramen and seven zombies prepared themselves.

9 p.m. Action. I went to East Finchley station and watched possible-Cyclopses coming out. She arrived only a few minutes late, which was a few minutes of thinking that she wouldn't turn up. I didn't know that I'd expected her to be wearing all black and to talk in a hoarse-grave voice until she turned out completely different. She dressed in light colours, her hair was blonde and she talked with a soft cadence. We went to a pub for a drink. I gave her two bags of picnic stuff to carry and made the unfortunate comment (in the light of what was about to take place) that I like to give heavy bags to my dates to carry because it makes it harder for them to run away.

Though I was still a little wrecked, I enjoyed talking to Cyclops in the pub so much that I wanted to call off the stunt. But, believing that she'd enjoy the planned date and that it was now the only way to meet her request, I ignored my nagging doubt and told her it was time to go to our date destination, and that she could call it off any time she wished. At least I felt secure in the knowledge that this was actually far safer than anything she'd thought I was planning or than something some real nut on the site might have planned to meet her request. On the bus, I sent a text to Paul to tell him we were on our way.

9.45 p.m. We entered the cemetery and walked along the path until gravestones started appearing. We followed the route that Paul had planned and turned right at a small church. The cemetery had no lighting and the darkness had descended with heavy and thorough prowess. We stopped to study a grave immersed in flowers. Someone had taken a great deal of time over arranging the display. Somehow, we had passed the point where we should have come off the path, but it was too dark to see the grave that was supposed to be my marker. I turned on my torch. The batteries were dead. I walked up and down, realising that the plan was off and that somewhere in this graveyard were a bunch of zombies who'd wait a long time for nothing to happen.

'Let's just go that way,' she said, pointing in a direction I knew to be wrong.

'But there's a path over here somewhere,' I stumbled.

'Can't we just sit anywhere and have our picnic?' she asked quite reasonably.

'No. I mean, yes, of course we could. But ... I found a nice picnic spot earlier when I was taking a walk.'

'Let's find another good picnic spot.'

'Yes, you're right.'

'So why are you still looking for your path?'

'It's just a bit of a challenge and I can't run from a challenge that easily,' I told her, acting like I had an obsessive disorder. 'I know it's around here somewhere.'

'I can't see any path,' she assured me.

I knew roughly the direction we should go in, but there was dense woodland between us and the zombies. 'It's definitely this way,' I said in as confident and relaxed a manner as I could muster.

We walked through dense wood in the dark in the enormous, empty cemetery. She showed no fear. I wondered if she was intending to rape me.

Soon we came out into the designated area and started to lay out the pathetic attempt at a picnic. She spotted a red light some distance away.

'It's probably a reflection of some kind,' I said, feeling as pathetic as the picnic food I'd grabbed.

'It looks like a night-camera light,' she observed astutely. I made a show of going over to check, loudly warning any ghosts to stay back, and hoping Paul would realise we could see his camera's recording light. It went out.

Back at the picnic spot, I continued opening the bags, while explaining that the light must have been a reflection after all. I brought out a couple of masks for us to wear, saying they'd add to the atmosphere. One of them broke straight away and the other one looked too silly, so we put them aside. I set out some candles and cloves of garlic around our picnic area to keep the spirits at bay.

'There's that red light again,' said Cyclops. This time she insisted on coming with me to check it out. The light went out again. I told her that the heavily treed area we were looking into was fenced off and that it must be someone's garden.

We returned to the picnic area. I opened and poured the champagne. We sipped.

She spotted another red light in a different bush. She had a theory, 'Maybe it's the cemetery's security system. I spotted a sign on the way in that says they have one.'

I agreed enthusiastically that she must be right. I suggested a card trick.

'One minute,' she said. 'That security light's moving round that bush.'

I turned to see a red light moving round a bush, and turned back, claiming not to have seen anything. I suggested a card trick more urgently. She suggested I check out the moving red light more urgently.

I went over to the light. She followed a safe distance behind. She spotted a figure moving, mentioned it and returned to the picnic area.

I spotted the silhouettes of two zombies moving out of the way of the night-vision camera light. She picked up her bag.

'It's OK,' I told her as calmly as I could. 'I tried to plan a date for you that would comply with your request. Sit down and I'll explain everything.' She sat. I explained that she was right about the cameras and that there were other people around, but they were all friends of mine and they just wanted to give her an unusual date that would be fun. They were going to come out and do a dance for her.

'I was just trying to impress you,' I told her pathetically.

She didn't believe me.

I stood up and shouted for camera people and zombies to come forth. Nothing happened.

Cyclops folded her arms and raised her eyebrows.

I shouted again. 'We've been sussed. Everyone come out now.'

Zombies appeared and shuffled toward us, doing awkward zombie-movements, uncertain whether to go on playing the part or not – if I hadn't been concerned over Cyclops's reaction to all this, the apologetic zombie-walks would have had me roaring with laughter because it was one of the funniest things I'd ever seen. One of them kept saying, 'You chose the ace of diamonds.' They looked great, considering the minuscule amount of time Carol had had to prepare them. The group consisted of Matt, Nick, Kirsty, Megan, Richard, Carol and finally, Papa CJ, whom I hadn't met before. Apparently, Matt rang him during the afternoon and said, 'Will you dress as a zombie tonight and come and scare a girl in a graveyard?' He said, 'Yes.' Paul and Jay (our second cameraman) came forward with their cameras, shaking their heads.

I think I was more embarrassed than anyone else and yet I was also amused that a group of grown adults were standing around a grave in make-up trying to impress my date.

Cyclops was such a mix of confused, amused, impressed and

unimpressed that her reactions were stifled for some minutes. We all picked at the pathetic picnic, passed the champagne and told Cyclops stories of the day that had just been. In the overcast sky, the full moon – the reason for making the date on this night – couldn't be seen.

The pubs were closed by now, so we went back to the house for a drink, and to my delight Cyclops joined us. We giggled over the magnificence of the fiasco. Matt said he'd been expecting Cyclops to slap my face and say, 'You're just like all the other boys.' Jay thought it would have been funny if, when I shouted for everybody to come out, other zombies we didn't know about had appeared, along with someone in a gimp mask. Paul described the date as 'Seven zombies around a gravestone apologising to a slightly embarrassed girl.' Cyclops said how relieved she'd been that there were girls in our group. She showed us a card trick – and not a bad one. She told me she'd see me again – Result! I called a taxi for her and soon after she'd gone I received a text giving me ten out of ten for effort.

I liked Cyclops. Her views interested me and I wanted to get to know her better on a more normal evening, but I'd been worried about whether she'd give me another chance. Now, here she was saying she would.

Jennifer

A ringing sound turned out to be the doorbell, which explained why it didn't stop when I turned off my alarm and punched it a few times. I wrestled my way out of a deep sleep and out of bed. As I approached the door, wearing a robe and a lopsided morning-face that held a cigarette, I woke up to the realisation that it was my lunch date. I apologised for oversleeping and sat her in the lounge while I went off to dress.

I quickly turned on the computer to see if there was an email from Cyclops concerning the date. There was. It raised worries that my intentions had been insincere and that I had set her up just to get copy for the book and my show. I had no time to respond because I had a date waiting in the lounge.

Jennifer apologised for her slightly erratic driving as we travelled to the restaurant, because she'd only recently passed her test – on the fifth attempt. We had a good meal and she told me a hilarious story of a date she'd been on with a man who made a strange noise after everything he said. She also told me of a stunt that happened in America. Some men encouraged a girl to climb into a coffin for a joke, and she successfully sued them for psychological damage.

Jennifer was great company and made me laugh loads. I told her I would see her again at gigs and at our parties.

I rushed home to write a reply to Cyclops. I emphasised that the stunt had been under control; I pointed out things she'd said in her emails which had suggested she wanted something of that ilk and reasons why I hadn't expected a graveyard to scare her. I told her that, if anything, I'd expected her to be disappointed because it wasn't as dangerous as she'd seemed to mean. And I assured her that I liked her and that she came before the book. I meant all of it.

Shooting out late to my second blind date of the day, I no longer felt in the mood for dating.

Emma

Emma had been put forward by a lady called Karen, who'd booked me for a gig in Phoenix. Emma turned out to be twenty-nine and very attractive, with eyebrows that moved independently and were capable of multitudinous charming expressions. We had a drink and wandered off to find some form of entertainment or a good restaurant. As we passed the Comedy Store, a man tried to sell us tickets. Well, I couldn't help telling Emma that we could get into this prestigious club for free. She was clearly interested. It felt a bit corny showing off like that, but I also thought it would be fun to go to the Comedy Store, especially as she'd never been there before. The bouncer, Julian, greeted me and invited us in. It was a quality show and afterwards, of course, I took Emma backstage to meet the comedians and introduced her to Don Ward, The Boss.

We had a good evening, and though I didn't feel that Emma fancied me, she did, voluntarily, say that she'd have another date with me, which was a very satisfying thing to hear from such an attractive lady.

I dashed home to see if Cyclops was still upset with me. It turned out that she hadn't been upset in the first place. She told me I was being overcautious with her humour. She'd enjoyed the date and wanted to see me again.

I caught a plane to the Isle of Man for a gig, and a date. My friend Rob, who hails from the island, had found me the date by asking his brother who asked his girlfriend who asked her friend Claire. I don't normally have people going so far out of their way to organise dates for me, but this had started to seem like normal behaviour since commencing my mission born of genius.

Claire

Claire met me at an Italian restaurant. She was funny and fun. You can be fun without being funny but you can't be funny without being fun. We had a great meal and talked through many subjects. She has a son who she says behaves a little effeminately, which is funny (and therefore fun) because he is called Stan the Man from the Isle of Man (I don't think that's his legal name). I enjoyed Claire's company and she came on to the club with me afterwards and then Claire, Rob's brother, Andy and his girlfriend, Sam, the other comedians and I went on for a drink afterwards. The date was a pleasure, and I think Claire was happy to be taken out to dinner by a man and then taken on to a comedy night, but she had no intention of marrying me.

End-of-April Report

I had thirteen arranged dates and ten mini-dates at gigs in April, plus a second date with Loki. In all, I was up to forty-two dates. Of the mini-dates, the shortest was fifteen minutes and the longest was fifty minutes. Four of the ten were with girls whom I would love to see again but none were with girls whom I thought would make me an ideal wife. The dating had started to affect my performances, firstly because I was getting drunk a lot (I don't normally drink much at a gig and can often go for weeks without alcohol. But the majority of dates like you to have a drink with them); secondly because at any one time I had a date with me and no thinking time before going on stage.

There had been twenty-two gigs in April all over the place. I wasn't taking any new gigs, but unfortunately my diary was packed with long-standing bookings which mostly couldn't be cancelled.

My life had become inordinately dishevelled. It was some time since I'd had a clear day to myself for basic things like paying bills, seeing friends and family, washing clothes, or tidying my room. I'd spent all my time travelling around for gigs, going on dates, writing a show, writing diary pieces that would later be condensed into a book, dealing with a pile of the Edinburgh red tape that goes with organising a show, and writing to women. The gig coming up in Phoenix was a magic performance, which is something I used to do and was extremely out of practice at – just another of many things to get around to.

I came home from most dates late or drunk or both and in no fit state to achieve a whole lot. Despite being in no fit state, I'd taken to entrenching myself at my computer until about 7 a.m. whenever I was home, and writing sleepy emails. Some were to new possible-wives I'd found on the internet. Most were to women whom I'd arranged dates with for some time in the future and whom I didn't want to lose by ignoring them until the date, to women I'd gone out with already and who'd become friends or whom I wanted to see again, and to women I hadn't yet found a space in the diary to fix a date with but once again didn't want to lose through neglect as I'd lost Amy.

Emily still reigned supreme, though I'd had only one date with her. We spoke regularly on the phone. She complained that I hadn't arranged a zombie dance for her.

Cyclops I wanted to see again. We hadn't had long to talk on our fiasco-date, and I wanted to know more about the things she wrote about in her profile.

There was also promise with Jode in Prague, but I hadn't seen her for some time and couldn't predict how well we'd get on when I eventually got round to visiting her (I knew we'd get on well, but would we get on well enough to marry?).

There had been one major change in my mission. From the moment it rocketed away from the launchpad, I'd started to enjoy the flight and I was beginning to look forward to the destination. Dating is fun. I began to believe that I really could find my ideal partner this way, and the thought of coming out of all this married to a woman who was just as amused as I'd be by how it happened seemed attainable and appealing.

However, despite all my efforts it was impossible to keep up with all the writing. It had also been impossible to work through my list of items that would make me eligible. Still, if I could propose to someone in May, then I could start working on the list, the book and the show.

MAYHEM OF MAY

I had a new communication from Cyclops. She was good about my absence in writing, saying that at least I was busy collecting her dowry. Part of her email included some questions that she needed answers to before we could marry. She asked how active my sperm are, and I replied that they must be pretty active because I'd seen them jump right over a magazine.

Emily rang. We chatted for an hour. I told her I could consider the possibility that we would wed. She told me she'd been thinking about it a lot. She could consider it, too.

I sent a text to Amy, and invited her and her boyfriend to a gig. After the show, Amy joined me at the bar and we talked about silly things, much as we'd done when we met. Her boyfriend came over to join us and told me he hated my act and didn't find it or me at all funny. I took him to one side and assured him that there was no need for jealousy because Amy and I were just friends, I hadn't known her long enough to fall in love with her, and I was happy for her if she'd found someone she loved. He didn't accept this, and told her that they were both leaving. Before leaving, he told me again that he hadn't laughed once at my act.

Rhiannon

An Irish girl with an exquisite laugh, which was provoked easily. We were on a mini-date by the bar at a gig in Bristol. She told me that she thought what I was doing was very romantic and that she loved the idea of a man searching for his ideal woman. She declared that all the female attention I was getting made me more attractive. She actually said, 'I don't find you all that good-looking but because you have all these women all over you I really want you.' I did have a large number of ladies around me discussing my mission. Rhiannon and I broke off from the group and had a date in a bar near the club, during which she continued to confuse me with insulting compliments.

I tentatively arranged to see her again but I also told her that there was a chance I'd already found my wife. I told her about Emily. Rhiannon laughed and told me not to be in too much of a rush. 'Your mission's young,' she said. 'I wouldn't start planning to settle down until it's at least a couple of months older.'

At another gig, I was accosted by a lady who'd heard me talk about my mission on stage and was disgusted.

'I don't know why you're doing it,' she said. 'You're not very attractive. I think you're ugly.' She pointed to another comedian. 'I'd go out with *him*.'

'But I wasn't asking you out,' I replied as I walked away.

The peculiar thing is that she contacted me through my web page and asked for a date. She even took the trouble to remind me where we'd met and of the conversation we'd had.

Two gigs in two towns later, back home, I answered a few emails and mostly spent the night writing apologies. Paige from America had been trying to ring me and had been sending me emails. I'd tried to reply whenever I could find a decent internet machine on my travels;

Mia had written some very sweet letters which I'd managed one quick reply to, and now her sweetness was wearing thin. Her last letter drew heavy attention to my rare responses.

After cancelling a gig the next day, I plonked myself in front of my computer with the intention of catching up with all my work. The first thing that happened was that I found an email from Cyclops which was very different in attitude from her last few emails. She said she'd been thinking about all this and decided that she was now angry with me. She told me that she had discussed it with friends who'd advised her that I was unethical in what I was doing. I wrote back, confused. She wrote back. I ended up calling her and we spoke for a long time. She argued that I was using women and taking advantage of their trust. I was misleading them and then going on stage and making fun of them. The women I was dating were the butt of my jokes.

She told me it was unethical for me to include people's writings in my book. In effect, she accused me of being nefarious and twisted. I told her that I had no intention of including anyone's letters unless they gave me express permission. The discussion became increasingly picky and I think – if I understood correctly – that she was demanding from me, in my work, the total confidentiality required by her own work – I can't tell you what her work is or she might sue me. But of course what I was doing was something completely different. I was going out on dates. I told her that I'd be using pseudonyms when required and altering other details so that I could give as honest an account as possible without infringing anyone's privacy.

I invited her to come to a preview of the show and see that the butt of all my jokes is not the women but myself, and I invited her to read what I'd so far written of the book. But she simply insisted that I was up to no good. We couldn't see eye to eye in the phone conversation and I was left feeling frustratingly misunderstood and down over what I was trying to achieve and what should have been fun.

All this had come out of nowhere and seemed to have been promoted by her friends' views. I didn't know if it would be possible to approach my mission differently, or how to be more honest with people if they were to feel abused by being mentioned by pseudonyms or by having their writings included, even though they had given express permission for me to do so.

Still, I did find out one thing from that conversation: Cyclops wasn't who or what I thought she was, and she wasn't what I was looking for in a wife. I wanted a girl with two eyes – both open. I felt conned by the claims she made in her profile – they didn't represent the kind of person who does what her friends tell her to do and who throws out accusations while refusing to look at the actual evidence. It's a shame I can't include her emails because they were funny and I think some of our banter showed a nicely developing relationship, which I was thoroughly into. But after I put down the phone I wasn't into it any more.

Lesson

I didn't agree with Cyclops's assessment of my mission. But I did realise that I'd been unduly enthusiastic. I made a note not to arrange any more outlandish first dates, no matter how well I thought they'd be received. I would get to know the girl first and not risk trusting her written description of herself.

Having said that, Cyclops's complaint wasn't about the date.

Until this point, I'd seen my mission as harmless fun which at best might lead to a real result, and at worst would just lead me back to where I was before. I didn't envisage any way that anyone except me could get hurt, especially as I'd kept to Jeff Cohen's advice and been straight with everyone. The accusation of being unethical took me totally by surprise, though I wasn't quite sure what it meant. Cyclops and her friends seemed to think I was merely dabbling with something which others took seriously. The truth was that this was the most serious thing I'd ever done in my life. But I had to make a greater effort to be ethical, even though I had no idea how to go about it.

In a sulk, I thought, Well, if people were going to accuse me of being unethical, I'd be properly unethical and marry a mail-order bride for a ha ha ending to my show.

Long Shots

Housemate Matt came into my room just as I was about to put an advert on a site which offered Chinese brides. The suggestion had come from possible-wife Loki, who'd heard that I was offering a free bicycle to whoever marries me. 'They love the bicycle in China,' she told me.

Matt and I were pretty tired and emotional when we constructed the following advert (we now regret it):

> I am a comedian writing a show and a book about my attempt to find myself a wife this year. I am a traditional Western man who lives in a traditional Western house.
>
> You must be able to use traditional Western cutlery, as is the Western tradition in our traditional Western house.
>
> Please include a photo of you with a fork in your hand.
>
> You must be able to defend me against my enemies in both armed and unarmed combat, using Western cutlery, as is the traditional Western tradition in our traditional Western house.
>
> Please include a photo of you with a fork in your hand in a defensive stance.
>
> If you marry me, I will buy you a bicycle.

I received eighty replies in a week and they have continued to trickle into my mailbox ever since.

Now, one problem with internet dating sites is that some of them use the sort of shark tactics and cons that I mentioned earlier. The Chinese site worked that way. I received emails telling me that Chen, Xiao, Vergie etc had contacted me but the only way to view the full response was by paying up, which I refused to do, firstly because the website was running a scam, and secondly because I couldn't face the guilt of finding umpteen pictures of Chinese women holding cutlery in defensive stances.

So the Chinese website didn't find me a bride, but the next day, again at about 5 a.m., Matt stood next to me as I joined a site offering Russian brides. The site asked me to describe my ideal wife so we wrote:

My ideal wife will be able to talk Russian, will not be a spy, will want to have sex under a capitalist regime, will drink vodka, like queuing for bread, and think a Big Mac is a luxury item.

I received a large number of replies. These ladies were so sexy that I felt wrong asking them to marry me in order to gain a free bicycle (which by now had become an on-going offer). Most of the girls were in their early twenties and very beautiful.

There was dazzling-blonde Olga. She wrote a several-page email, which included a sentence in the first paragraph stating that she did not drink, smoke or take drugs. I didn't read the rest. There was a beautiful Elina in a bikini, a dark-haired and sophisticated young Anastasiya, an Anna to die for, a pretty Yuliya with seductive blue eyes and another Olga who was attractive, with a lot of attitude on her face. She wrote:

Hi Carey

It was nice to read your profile. Nice to know that you are a creative man. Me too and i am a hooligan, used to work in international concert agency in Moscow (i am a native dweller of Moscow) engaged in bringing pop and rock singers and some shows to Moscow now i work for record company.

I would be nice to learn about you more maybe we become good friends.

drop me a line, ask me questions

Take care

Olga

P.s a song for you: I want to ride my bicycle i want to ride my bike :)))))))))))))))

Friends warned me about Russian brides: it's a scam to get money off Western men; they're only after green cards and work permits; they aren't sexually liberated like Western women; they want Western men because Russian men treat them badly.

I wanted to investigate for myself so I sent the girls that looked interesting a questionnaire raising these concerns.

I received a few unhelpful replies, a couple of rude ones, and one from Olga the 'hooligan' (I expect that was a mistranslation, but maybe not). Her replies were heavily sarcastic but she clearly had great humour, which caught my attention.

I used 'green card' for simplicity as I expected these Russian ladies were mostly talking to Americans and would relate to the term better than trying to relate to a particular type of visa. (I have left in Olga's original spellings and punctuation because I like it that way).

Q: You are obviously very beautiful and selling yourself short. So what do you stand to gain?

A: Selling is an offensive word, it is a pitty that western men are so shortminded to think about russian girls only in this way. I want to get the bicycle you promised. I have always dreamt to sell myself to a man from london for a bicycle.

Q: Are things so bad over there?

A: Yes and no as in every country including yours at least our country wont be under the water some day as your Kent and other lands

Q: Why do you want to marry a man from the West?

A: I want to be a married girl some day and it doesnt matter if it is a man from east or west or from Antarctica he must be cool

Q: Why do you want to leave Russia?

A: It is always hard to leave a native land. Russian girls have a special soul and if they ever married a foreign man they are unhappy as a rule and they come back home cause it is special spirit in Russia calling them back. One should live here for some years to understand it. A lot of foreign men who have been working in Russia for some years become addicted to Moscow or Russian life, lots of them leave there wifes and children at the end and stay here. After fucking Russian girl it becomes very difficult for them to fuck again their crooked wifes

Q: Are you just after a green card?

A: Of cause, first i will find an old ugly wrinkled rich man, seduce him, let him merry me and make me a green card then i will be fucking him hard every night and very soon he will die from heartattack and all his money and property will be mine.

Q: Will you run off as soon as you have your green card?

A: Of cause, and then i will be spending all the money from my latest husband with my young russian lover

Q: How can we meet?

A: I will send you an invitation, you will go to Russian embassy and will easily get a visa or you can buy a tour my dear. Dont forget to bring a bicycle.

Q: How do Russian men treat you?

A: They usually hang me with my arms in handcuffs on the big iron hook for three days, feed me with dogflesh and dont give water. Will you rescue me my knight?

Q: And, here is a delicate question that you do not have to answer: I am told that Russian women are not sexually liberated like Western women. Is this true?

A: The truth is that most of western women look like carrion-crows they dont shave their arm pits and legs and how you poor western men fuck them i wonder.
WHY THERE ARE SO FEW QUESTIONS FROM YOU? I WANT TO TELL YOU MORE
Say hello to the big ben
All the best
Olga

We started writing to each other. In her second email she asked how I saw our first meeting. I wrote some story about her crying in the freezing cold beside a market stall that sold jeans and wishing that she could buy a pair. I turn out to be the stallholder, which she realises when I remove my fur hat. We dance all over Russia and are invited to the Kremlin to dance. I then asked her some more questions. Here they are, with her answers.

Q: Do you already have children?

A: None

Q: What does your mother think of you marrying an Englishman?

A: She is thinking!

Q: What does your father think of what your mother thinks of you marrying an Englishman?

A: My father thinks that if my mother is still able to think this is already good!

Q: What does you brother think of you marrying an Englishman?

A: My brother thinks as my mother do

Q: How big is your brother?

A: 35 this summer

Q: What does you sister think of you marrying an Englishman?

A: Havent got any sisters

Q: What is your favourite Chinese food dish?

A: A duck quack-quack-quack-quack

Q: How old are you?

A: 27 in August

Q: Can you spell the English word orthochromatic?

A: Give me a call and I will easily do it

Q: Can you ride a bicycle?

A: Long time ago in the Pioneer camp. Will you remind me how to do it my knight?

In another email I asked if I could include snippets of hers in my book. She replied, 'I will give you a permission in case you confirm me that your next book will be written about me with the title *The Best Wife In The World – Is My Wife.*'

Through a batch of emails after those I became very fond of Olga and wanted to meet her. My idea for a show had been somewhat crazy; perhaps the denouement would be just as unexpected. I would go to Russia and meet Olga.

I wrote to her asking if she'd ever had a man travel to Russia just to see her for a few minutes. In her reply she wrote, 'It has never happened to me before that someone comes to Moscow just to have a glance at me so the thing you said flatters me so much.'

The system for getting a Russian tourist visa is complicated. I had to book the hotel room, and then wait for confirmation of the booking from the hotel to reach an agency in Russia, which would then send me a tourist visa invitation, which I was to take to the Russian embassy. The hotel confirmation, I was told, would take about twenty-four hours.

But, several days later I still hadn't received the invitation and I also had problems with the internet agency arranging the flights because they hadn't confirmed my booking. I wasted a day emailing these various groups, trying to find out what was going on.

Eventually, the flights were confirmed but the hotel still wasn't. The agency assured me they'd receive confirmation any moment. The next morning was my last chance to get the visa.

I'd been up all the previous night at the computer, pressing the damned Refresh button. I kept writing emails to the Russian agency telling them that if they didn't get the invitation to me by the end of the afternoon it would be too late.

At end of business, the Russian agency wrote to tell me that my request for accommodation had been refused. The hotel had given no explanation.

All our email exchanges had led to this dead end, thanks to an incompetent hotel manager. If he'd turned down the booking days earlier, I'd have had time to do something about it. But now it was too late.

I'd really been looking forward to meeting Olga. I posted a letter to the Russian embassy telling them my feelings.

Dear Russia,

Just like other people born in Britain, I am a British Citizen. And just like all British Citizens who have wanted to visit you, I have too. Recently, a very exciting opportunity to do just that occurred. Today, however, that opportunity has been lost, but not, I feel, in an honourable way as a chess player may lose to a better player. It was more similar to a chess player losing to a boxer, most particularly if we imagine that this analogous game was meant to be a friendly and that the boxer replied to 13 N-QN5 in the Nimzowitsch defence with a knockout punch.

I am writing a show for the Edinburgh Festival and a commissioned book called *Marry Me* about my attempt to find my ideal partner and marry her this year. One woman I have been writing to is Russian and lives in Moscow.

My show is a romantic show about love, and where better to visit on a quest for love than your romantic city of Moscow? I think of Red Square as a big red pumping heart that's square-shaped and the Kremlin as romantic in its own way. I would have been travelling to you tomorrow to meet this beautiful girl in your beautiful city. But alas, it is now not to be.

I booked the hotel and received an email from the hotel stating that I would receive a notification, which would allow the booking agency in Moscow to send me a tourist invitation and voucher that I needed to enter you. I also filled out a visa request form. I have waited patiently by my computer since then for this invitation. I read up on Russian life, drank vodka and learnt a little Cossack dancing so that I would fit in. But like a new love full of promise that is not quite as it seemed our relationship has ended with this letter born of a broken heart and me being five hundred quid out of pocket because the flight tickets cannot be redeemed.

The manager of the hotel I was booking through kept the agency waiting until the last minute today to turn down my request for a room without any explanation. If his hotel had been too full, he could have told me immediately so that I could have made other arrangements. Instead, he has made it impossible for me to gain a visa in time for my trip. I cannot imagine any motivation for the hotel manager's behaviour other than jealousy.

I tried gaining advice but there was no method of gaining a

visa in time. They say that love conquers all and yet it seems that love is easily defeated by a jealous hotel manager. Though I am sure that the traditional Russian punishment of sending people to Siberia is now out of date and considered too harsh for most crimes, I would feel a little better about this ugly turn of events if the hotel manager in question were to be sent there at least long enough for him to think about what he has done.

You could have been the happy moment in a show that is receiving a lot of press coverage. My show could have put Russia on the map. Instead, Russia shall be remembered as a place of cold winters and alcohol abuse. Yet, I feel no bitterness toward you. Just disappointment in you. So, adios Russia, mon amigo. Perhaps, one day our paths will cross again and next time you will open your arms to me and embrace me like the friend I offered to be.

13 N-QN5. Your move . . .

IS THIS ROMANTIC?

Before a gig at the Belfast Empire, I had a blind date set up by my friend Janice. The date was with a girl called Sofia. Sofia is from Greece and was a pleasant surprise from the word go. I wanted to do the occasional blind date on my search because it was always possible that I was failing to find my wife by looking only at girls who happened to have a number of characteristics that I thought I was looking for. Sofia had told me that she would be wearing a red scarf. As I hung around waiting for her, everyone decided to put on red scarves and walk past me. The most attractive of the red-scarf passers-by was my date.

I discovered that I'd rushed out without my wallet and started the date by asking Sofia to buy me a drink.

We went for a quick Chinese meal before the gig. We discussed my mission and whether it was romantic.

'If this all goes the way it seems to be going,' I told her, 'my wife and I will have a book on our coffee table all about the way we met. Maybe she'll write the last chapter. My wife will actually be the happy ending in a story. That's romantic, isn't it?'

'Yes,' said Sofia. 'That's very romantic.'

'But, there's another side to the argument: my wife will have a book on her coffee table about all the girls I've gone out with this year. And it won't be a very lavish honeymoon because I've spent all my money on other women.'

'Hmmm. That's not so romantic.'

We reached the same conclusion: that the mission was romantic and unromantic all at the same time and would sway more to one side depending on how it developed.

Sofia poured the Chinese tea. The waiter came over to serve the meal and was momentarily confused to find that the food bowls on our table were full of tea. He removed the empty teacups, leaving an embarrassed Sofia giggling with her head in her hands; her giggle was infectious. She asked if I was going to mention in the book that she'd poured the tea into the bowls. I told her I had no choice. She accepted this with some amusement, although I suspected Cyclops would have called it unethical.

My mobile phone rang, and I ignored it because I was on a date but then I realised that it might be to do with the gig. I played the message and it turned out that I was supposed to be on stage. I think this is a compliment to Sofia which she should see as compensation for mentioning the tea incident – I was enjoying her company so much that I forgot I should be doing a gig.

We raced round to the Empire. It was a fantastic gig and I mentioned Sofia during it, though I didn't point her out. We continued drinking afterward. Sofia was a superb date. It was relaxing and fun and I think we got on splendidly. She gave a great hug. But there was no vibe that we were going to marry.

> ## Lesson
>
> I reached a new resolve about continuing on these sorts of
> date. In those halcyon pre-mission days, I would have bent
> over backwards to see a girl like Sofia again. Now time was
> bearing down on me.

Dawn

She'd seen me at a comedy club in Birmingham and contacted my
website. In her email, she offered to send me a picture and tell me
more about herself, and she included some dates when she'd be in
London. I called the phone number in her message and arranged to
see her immediately, because immediately was the only date on her
list that I could do. This would be my first totally blind date, in that
Dawn hadn't so much as been recommended by anyone and I had no
idea what she looked like, how old she was, or anything else that
might be relevant.

Dawn turned out to be twenty-six, and her personality was a
pleasant kind of odd. She was a little taller than me. She had very
long black hair, a youthful face with inviting, full lips – which is not,
as she put it, a euphemism for 'fat lips' – and green eyes. She was very
sexy. I couldn't understand how I was meeting so many sexy women.
She originally came from an area of London's East End that I didn't
know and she spoke in a broad cockney accent which sounded as if
she was parodying herself as her tongue hurdled consonants, half-
nelsoned vowels and disrespected syllables. In the East End, most
names seem to follow a one-syllable rule and become Tel, Del, Mel,
Kel, Dave, Bob, Bill, Sel, Sal, Cole, etc. My name was no exception.
After asking the correct pronunciation of my name, Dawn came out

with the glorious sentence, 'Carey? That's a lovely name, Kel.' And I remained Kel for the evening.

She told me she'd been so amused by what I was up to that she couldn't help but contact me. She also told me that she was very religious and then, without pausing for breath, asked what I thought of her boots. I said they were nice. She asked if I knew what kind of boots they were. I said no. She said, 'Fuck me boots.' I said I'd try if she really wanted me to but that I expected the openings would be too large to give me much pleasure. I wasn't particularly proud of that joke, which was good because she ignored it and told me she'd worn the boots especially for this occasion and was telling me what they meant in case I failed to work it out for myself. Tsk! Women! Only interested in one thing. Did no one believe in marriage any more?

Apart from some nagging doubts installed in my brain by Cyclops, and constant tiredness through constant lack of sleep, I was quite happy with the way things were going. I'd met some great women and had some fabulous dates. But I'd expected my search to bring out all the so-called 'nice romantic girls'. Not that the girls I'd met weren't nice and romantic, but it turns out that these traits are far from exclusive. I wasn't complaining. I'd never had so much female attention in my life.

Back home, I wrote all night. The dates I'd arranged would run dry in three weeks' time because I'd been writing to girls I was already in contact with, not finding new possible-wives. If things didn't work out with Emily I'd be back to square one and with no one else as promising on the horizon.

At around 11 p.m. my friend Susan popped round. Since word had spread about my mission, I'd discovered that many people around me were on these dating sites. I'd been asking women for the female perspective. Generally, they seem to answer emails more than initiate correspondence, and they have to wade through plenty of nutters. Most do not check their inboxes as frequently as I would have liked, which may explain why so many of my emails didn't receive a reply, not even one telling me where to go. Susan had a theory that this kind of dating takes away an advantage that is normally afforded to women when they meet a man because women size men up quickly, and in letter-form he's able to be deceitful in a way that he wouldn't achieve face to face.

Susan showed me an email she'd received from a man who said very nice things about where he was living and where he had lived. He said that the people he worked with were all a bit fake and that he wanted to meet some normal people. He told her that she was cute. Then he told her that he loved her hair. Then he finished the letter by saying, 'Do you fancy a shag?'

I sent a text to the lovely Emma who I had taken to the Comedy Store and told her that I had great admiration for her eyebrows, which each have a different character and that she should give them individual names. She replied that they are now called Gin and Tonic to remind her of our evening.

I hadn't heard from Meganetta, the very tall girl, for some time so I wrote her a note saying I hadn't forgotten her. She replied:

Hello Carey,

No, I've not forgotten you either! How could I? Fabulous emails and a great personality.

No, I've just been busy being a bit of a tart! Know this about me now! I've been living this year based on not dissimilar principles to you, but actually, meeting up with three different guys this month has not been easy and it's left me feeling exhausted and fake. They've all been really nice but only one of them's really fun and he's married!

So I've devised rules for myself now.

1. Take a break from physically meeting up, keep emailing.

2. When the meeting up moment comes, don't do dinner at his place (makes you feel obliged to share his bed and despite him saying that he won't "do anything", I usually can't trust myself!)

3. Wear really awful undies (the only way to ensure that the jeans stay firmly on!)

4. DO something on the date other than just dinner or coffee (this somehow feels like an hour or so of interrogation where the conclusion either has to be, let's get married tomorrow or let's never speak again ever!)

5. Don't treat it like a date.

God I really sound pissed off with the whole thing don't I?

Just know that you're a breath of fresh air, but leave me a while before we meet up. Need to keep reading your great emails. Tell me about any meetings you've had so far.

Meganetta

I replied:

Meganetta,

That's hilarious. Your sentiments reflect exactly where I am at but it is much harder for me to slow down on the dating because of this blasted show/book I'm writing, and it's hard to find my future wife without meeting any women. When I finally meet you, it will be the first time I will have made a girl happy by buying her a present of extremely un-sexy lingerie. Having said that, and whilst I respect your realisation that you need to slow down on the 'tarting', I would have preferred you to realise this after our date (though not because of it).

Anyway, how about this: what if I promise you a date that will have nothing to do with sex (if we get on great, there'll be plenty of time for that later), and only a few minutes of interrogation over a drink. Let's go and do something grand fun that we would not normally do. For this I will need to know what you don't normally do. ie if I arrange to take you on a barge down the Thames that is rowed by a Venetian man, whilst we both experiment our way through a huge batch of different ice-creams, it would be a great shame to find out that you do that kind of thing every weekend. I would be surprised though because I do not think they allow barges on the Thames. Or Venetians (they sing too much). Very dangerous.

Obviously, it would take a long time for you to list all the things that are grand fun that you do not normally do, so I'll just make suggestions and you add to them or reject them as you wish and we will choose the best when it comes close to the date. Thus, I would suggest we set a date for our date in about a month's time, so that the pre-date date-plan game may commence.

Here's my first suggestion: a picnic in a hot-air balloon. I have no idea how to go about arranging such a thing but I will look into it. Are you afraid of heights? (Please don't take that question personally. I don't mean to still be going on about the height thing.)

Before I went to bed, I sent an email to Loki explaining why I'd been so remiss at contacting her — a subject she'd raised in an email in which she suggested that I buy her presents instead.

I've got three white stress hairs, which I'm grateful for because I'm using them to prove to people that I really am this busy. None of it's going all that amazingly because I'm so busy having to keep up with all the different facets of this project. The broken toilet in our house is still broken and apparently there are mushrooms growing in there now; the electricity in my room has gone mad and I'm working in the dark; the mess in my room is now ankle high; all bills are red going on bailiff; a gym gave me free membership for a week and I didn't manage to go along for even one session; I'm eating terribly and sleeping less than any doctor would recommend; my computer has caught a virus that my virus-software is not recognising and I have to re-run internet software every time I want to check my emails; when I check my emails there are lots of complaints from people whom I have not got back to, and I'm supposed to be getting a magic show ready for Phoenix.

And I explained that one of the main reasons I couldn't call people back efficiently was because I was travelling around too much. Mobiles don't work on the Underground, and calls on trains are no good because they constantly get cut off and if the train's busy a long call can be uncomfortable. I couldn't make romantic calls when travelling in someone else's car because that's rude and awkward. And making calls to other girls while out on dates is very hard indeed to justify.

Three hours later, I woke and checked my email accounts. Loki hadn't exactly taken my whingeing seriously, which I could tell by the way she replied by turning my words into a poem.

My friend Ronnie rang. 'I've heard how your mission's going. You lucky bastard,' he said.

'You don't understand, Ronnie. It's exhausting. I can't get off the phone. I don't even have time to talk to you now 'cos there's women I have to ring back.'

'You lucky bastard.'

Back in London, I had a quick drink in the pub with a friend of mine called Tessa and told her I was getting too run-down to carry out my mission efficiently.

'Most people take a few months off to write a book,' she said.

'I know. I'm trying to write a book and a show and a million emails and go on dates and perform all over the place, and even though all these women are being nice they're also really demanding. I can't keep up any more. I'm spread so thin you wouldn't be able to taste me in a sandwich.'

'Cancel gigs.'

'I've cancelled as many as I could, including some in a ski resort. I'm beginning to upset people and don't want all this to end with me failing to find a wife and no one wanting to employ me.'

She put an arm round me and I think she was about to say something comforting when my phone on the table in front of us beeped. One of the girls I'd seen recently had sent me a picture of her breasts. Tessa removed her arm and said, 'It's hard to feel sorry for you really.'

We both giggled and I fell asleep on her lap in the pub.

SEX WITH THE DEVIL

By now, everywhere I went people were talking about my wife-finding mission. I discussed it in comedy club dressing rooms, on stage with audiences, at the bar after the gig with audience members, during car journeys to and from gigs, and in every other social situation that came up. The pain of my dislocated shoulder had increased because of all the slaps on the back I received from people admiring my work.

Discussing the mission brought me many other offers of dates.

I paid particular heed to advice from women but also had a problem with the type of details women wanted to hear about how my quest was going. Most of them egged me on to tell them very personal details of the women I was seeing. 'That's what women want to hear,' said one of them. 'Read our magazines. Women want to see other women with food round their mouths pulling embarrassing expressions and with their crotches showing.'

'My kind of women don't buy those magazines,' I said.

'No. But they'll still have a look,' she said. 'You should be reporting everything you get up to with everyone. Dish the dirt.'

I told her I wouldn't and couldn't, but I will tell you that I had a second date with the lascivious beauty known as Selina who at our last meeting had stripped off in Green Park.

After that second date, I started seeing her as the Devil and I told her so. She was leading me from the path of good. Under normal circumstances, I'd have perceived her as an angel. We had an amazing night which descended deep into the fiery pits of filthy-out-there-funny-experimental-credit-to-our-imaginations hell (where hell is not a bad thing), and it was the best of its kind, ever. But then I'd expect nothing less of the Devil. I knew she wasn't going to marry me. So why did I see her? If you met her, perhaps you'd understand. But, considering I had so little time to meet potential wives, it was foolish of me to waste time with a girl who didn't fit the criteria, even though she was happy to have my time wasted on her.

When I'm in a loyal relationship, I've always been honest and faithful. But as a single man I had every right to a good time.

Yes, but by spending a night with this temptress, I wasn't giving my project the sincerity it needed.

Hmmm, it is also true, though, that I had to investigate what I liked and what I hoped to find in a wife. Selina had some characteristics which fascinated me and which I'd love to find in my future spouse, so spending time with her was for the overall good of the project.

OK, that last paragraph didn't even convince me as a good argument. Selina was simply a Devil taking me away from my purpose with her great looks, youth, intelligence, wit, charm, and devious imagination.

I felt as if I was losing my mind. Believe it or not, these were the dark days. No one had much sympathy for my plight.

Lesson

Same as the last lesson about not arranging these sort of dates; but more so.

BACK TO THE MISSION

At a club called Up the Creek in Greenwich, I talked to a couple of girls who put themselves up as possible-wives. They had an argument over which of them was best suited for me. I thought they were joking until one of them hit the other. I slipped out of there and didn't know that someone else in the audience had taken note of my wife-search on behalf of a very cool friend called Jenni.

I spent the entire plane journey to Phoenix, Arizona, crushed between two bodybuilders whose shoulders overlapped my seat. Every time they stood up, I stood up too, even if I was asleep. I kept waking up in different parts of the aircraft.

Arizona was hot and it was beautiful. The gig itself was difficult. I was performing outside, which is not good for comedy, by a pool, which is not good for sound amplification quality, with difficult angles, which is not good for magic, to executives who had just arrived and many of whom had travelled long distances, which is not good for attention span, and most of whom did not know each other, which is not good for atmosphere, and they were all accountants and engineers, which is not good for entertainment. My case was smashed en route to Arizona (the airline replaced it), and some of my tricks were damaged. I also had some unexpected hitches on the day, which meant that I had to make some quite drastic changes to the act.

Most of the group were fun to hang with and appreciated the show. I went with them all into the Sonoran Desert where we admired saguaros (giant cacti), fired fake bullets from weird guns, roped metal cattle, ate steak and beans, and looked at stars through a powerful telescope.

Karen

On the first night in Arizona, Robin, the boss of the group and a very amiable man, suggested I have a date with Karen, the very attractive, sophisticated lady who'd booked me and who worked for the company organising the event. I said I'd love to have a date with Karen. She pointed out that it would be unprofessional for her to discuss such a thing while out in Arizona organising this event, and it would also be wrong, because she'd put her friend Emma up for a date with me, so the two of us sat up late drinking and discussing how we could not discuss it over several hours in what amounted to a date.

'There's a movie deal under discussion,' I told her. 'You might get a chance to choose who plays you. I'm going to be played by Brad Pitt.'

'In that case,' she replied, 'I will play me.'

Having agreed a future date with Karen it now seemed wrong to be also seeing her friend Emma so I took her off my list of second dates to arrange.

Home again, I faced the usual array of emails from women moaning about my inefficiency in replying to them. There was an email from Amy to say she was getting married. Apparently, her new boyfriend had asked for her hand on the night I'd last seen them both, when he told me he hated my act.

First Sarah, now Amy: two girls I'd dated were getting married. A new finale to my mission occurred to me: I don't find a spouse; everyone else does.

I got home to find Phil in the lounge. I told him how my mission was and wasn't going. He suggested that I go out with an extremely ugly girl and with some gay men, to show that I was open-minded and a nice person and so that I could investigate what I am and am not into. He assured me that this would be good for the story, but I remained convinced that he wanted me to do these things for his own amusement. And I was in no need of the suggested investigation, which anyway had a flaw in it. If I went out with an ugly girl to show myself as a nice guy, in order to show that properly, I'd have to write about how ugly she was. I didn't think that would be kind.

I travelled to Glasgow to perform for the next three nights. On the first night, I decided to go back to my hotel because I didn't want to meet any more potential wives. Another comedian called John did hang around and took the phone number of a potential wife and arranged a date with her. The girl's name was Kimberley. Feeling it would be immoral to let her down, I agreed to meet her.

On Friday, I had another couple of mini-dates at the gig, which went nowhere. One of them started criticising the act of a friend of mine who was stood next to us overhearing her and she tried to get out of this faux pas so badly it created a more hilarious faux pas in which she assured us both that she hadn't meant my friend.

Kimberley

My date with Kimberley was another blind one. I overslept. I rang her a few minutes after we were supposed to have met and suggested that she grab a coffee in the lobby of my hotel while I sorted myself out. I'd been late for most of my dates and had developed a number of ruses for dealing with it. On one occasion I ran into a pub late, and found the girl upstairs. She hadn't seen me so I went downstairs and sent her a text message asking how late she'd be. She came downstairs and apologised for waiting in the wrong part of the pub. I owned up and she was amused by the trick so I got away with the lateness. Another time I asked the girl if she was angry. She said no, so I took out a piece of paper and made a note of her reaction, explaining that it was one of the wife-tests and she'd passed.

Kimberley turned out to be great company from the word go. She was funny and interesting and she had great date-attitude on her. When I look out over an audience I can see the people who've come out to have a good time and the people sitting back with their arms folded, waiting to be impressed; the former tend to be the ones who enjoy their evening and are the most pleasurable to entertain. Similarly, I've found that the best dates are with girls who come out intending to enjoy themselves.

We had a coffee and discussed the idea of doing something exciting like a helicopter ride. One thing we had agreed is that we would avoid the football game (Arsenal v someone), which everyone seemed to be rambling on about because it was some kind of important game.

Kimberley and I visited a tourist centre to see if we could get some advice on helicopter rides. The first time I went to Glasgow, I got into a taxi and asked the driver about the local tourist attractions. He said he'd show me, so he drove me along a few streets that had little other than bars.

The tourist centre had very little to interest us but there was a helicopter ride on offer. This ride was way out of my financial league and I think it's obvious that the company offering the ride has a monopoly over what looks like the whole of Scotland. Instead, we went for a meal – the restaurant had the football on. We ate and left, deciding to try again to find some non-football things to do. We found a shop that sold funny sexy outfits. I had Kimberley try on a couple of funny outfits (nothing that rude).

Then Kimberley had a great non-football idea: we'd go and give blood. I agreed that a giving-blood-date would be a top idea, and off we went. We found the blood-donating place but it was closed. So we went to a pub, drank, and watched football.

My date with Kimberley was all fun and we agreed to see each other again but I had no hunch that we were heading for marriage.

I arrived home and howled with frustration over the problems with my computer. I rushed out for a date with a girl who didn't really have any romantic interest in me and just wanted sex. I felt like a piece of meat.

I turned down her offer, not because I'm an angel but because I'd hit a state of high stress from my workload, which was ever-mounting. But it did seem unfair, because my romantic life had been sad to non-existent before my mission and now I had a magnificent single life on a plate but no appetite to eat it.

As far as sex goes – and it would be rude not to mention it – I hadn't been bathing in some sybaritic pool of pleasure or acting the Lothario. It had happened on the odd occasion with a girl whom I'd come to like and who knew exactly what she was getting into. I'd been honest with everyone, as Jeff Cohen told me to be, though I doubt his advice was intended to extend beyond the date.

Back home, I called Emily and tried to move our next date forward. We eventually found a date we could both do. Then I succeeded in getting past a problem with my computer virus and opened my email account to discover a gig on the date I had just arranged that would not be cancellable.

I also found this in my email box:

Hello

My friends apparently consider me to be so utterly incapable of forming functional lasting relationships with the opposite sex they insisted I try emailing a stranger they saw on stage who's trying to get married for material. Naturally I jumped at the chance.

I'm a 30-year-old chain smoker. I live on an old canal boat as if I was brought up by wolves. I'm lazy, selfish and have quite a large nose. I have the demeanour and sometimes odour of a woman twice my age and regularly drink enough gin to kill a man. I'm quite a catch.

I do have some good qualities. I scrub up all right, I am generally kind to the old and infirm and sometimes I give to charity. I could really do with some funny at the moment so if you fancy a pint, please do get in touch. If not, bonne chance with the ladies.

kind regards

Jenni

I sent a reply saying that she must be as selfish as she claimed if she was taking up all that nose all by herself, and that I didn't know wolves had a reputation for living on old canal boats. I asked some other questions, to which she replied admirably, and she included a couple of photos. She looked very sexy.

Jenni the Boatgirl is attractive, dark-haired and about my height. We went for a meal and then she took me to see her boat. I was quite fascinated by her lifestyle on this boat. We talked for hours over wine and beer. She's quite sceptical and realistic about many things in ways that I admire. Jenni lives a very independent life. She is a realist. She appreciates good books and fine things. She has taste. It was a thoroughly enjoyable date and again there was promise in the air.

In her email to me she'd described herself as 'quite a catch' in a self-mocking manner, but I did actually find her quite a catch.

* * *

While catching a nice girl I also found time to catch a nasty cold. I'd been saying for a while that my mission seemed to be going the way of that film *Super Size Me*, in which a man eats too much McDonald's food and gets ill. I was getting ill from being involved with too many women. Among them were Caroline and Stella.

Caroline had read an article I had written, in a magazine called *Writers' Forum*, about my hunt for a wife. She was nice but I think I looked and acted like the victim of a cold and of a lot of stress. We did laugh a lot, though. She asked to meet again and if I'd been dating without intention I'd have agreed.

Stella had originally met me in a comedy club and now met me again in London. On this second meeting, she told me that she sold time-share properties for a living. We chatted, and casually disagreed on politics and morality. She smiled away our differences in a manner which inferred she was being generous. I shook my head at things she said, and I was being generous. She tried to sell me a time-share. Bye bye, Stella.

I quickly felt better about things when I turned my phone on and it was full of messages from my new female friends. I sent a text to Kimberley, whom I knew as Kimbo, and told her that her name was now Limbo because predictive-text recognises that word. If I could get all the women I was regularly texting to change their names to predictive-text-friendly names, I reckoned I'd save about an hour a week.

In the evening I performed a gig at a singles club and mistakenly thought it would be a good opportunity to test some of the material for my Edinburgh show. I had the impression that the club would be a regular group who enjoyed activities together. It was actually a group of people who were being brought together for the first time and seemed quite desperate to impress each other. Admittedly, my performance was terrible. My cold streamed out of my nose and I sniffled through emails and stories. The show didn't so much die as fail to spark, but it didn't make me feel good about its being ready for the Festival.

The audience seemed a little posh. They 'ooh'd a few times at bits that surprised me. They found a snippet of Paige too shocking. I think Paige is cool. Towards the end, I gave up and slipped into my normal set material, but that was also too shocking for them, which at least confirmed my view of the audience. As I looked over the group, I could see people I instantly respected, who didn't wait for approval to laugh at something. They had relaxed faces and sitting positions. Most others were uncomfortable. So many people are embarrassed about being themselves.

This level of embarrassment was the biggest surprise that I was constantly coming across on the dating scene. The most common conversation I had on dates was over what I could or couldn't say about them in the book I was supposed to be writing. This often came down to extreme trivia. One girl knocked a salt shaker over and was worried I'd mention her name and write some damning prose about how clumsy she was.

I quit smoking and travelled back to Birmingham for another gig. Quitting smoking was one of things that I'd put on the list of things I'd do by the time of the Festival to make myself as eligible as possible.

In Birmingham, I phoned one of my former dates and was on the phone for an hour and a half. Then another one rang and I complained to her that the other girl had kept me on the phone for an hour and a half. Her reaction? She was upset that I'd spoken to the other girl for an hour and a half when I'd been keeping my calls to her relatively short. We ended up talking for nearly two hours. Under normal circumstances, I'm not very sociable. I like social situations and I like to hear from friends; but give me the facts, exchange some humour, and say goodbye. I'd borrowed a laptop computer for the weekend so that I could try and write something, and I'd left the gig early so that I could come back to my hotel and make use of that computer, but by 2.30 a.m. I'd only been on my phone. At that point I was about to turn the phone off but it rang as I did. It was another potential wife I'd dated.

She asked me how writing the show was going. I told her I wasn't getting much done because I was being kept on the phone too long. She wanted, and then insisted on, more details so I told her that one problem was that I was now in contact with too many women, and though I kept trying to bring it down to a handful, even a handful are extremely time-consuming. I came off the phone to her at around 4 a.m. She spent much of the conversation being amused by my predicament and making suggestions for handling it, none of which included her saying goodbye. She suggested I write about how long she kept me on the phone.

Before leaving Birmingham, I had a daytime date with a girl called Bouncy. She was very bouncy. Her hair was big and bouncy. We had a nice meal but she admitted to finding my humour and thinking too dark. Her world is full of happy thoughts all written in pink. We had a laugh about our differences. It left neither of us offended and she said she was looking forward to seeing my show. And then she bounced off through the streets of Birmingham.

Lesson

I don't think what people describe as a dark sense of humour is usually dark. I think they're dark in their sensitivity and fear of laughing. I want a wife who'll laugh at any subject matter (so long as it is funny).

Emily: Second Date

Emily, the girl who'd been recommended by another girl I'd dated, the girl I fancied, the girl I would marry, rang to say that she wanted to see me. I cancelled a date with another girl and slotted Emily in for the next evening.

We drove around London in her car and decided to see if we could cross six bridges in thirty minutes. We gave up after one bridge, Tower Bridge, because she spotted a restaurant she liked.

During our meal, she told me that her friend Terry, whom I'd dated and who said she'd start dating more often as a result of our date, had indeed done just that: met a man, and got engaged. It was nice to know I was putting the idea of marriage in people's heads. Not marriage to me, unfortunately, but it was a start.

We sat in a candlelit corner. Emily is petite. She has long black hair and a nose which wriggles when she giggles. She works as a freelance journalist and she plays bass in a band. We agreed on choices of books, on art, on science, on humour, on food, on movies, on everything. She told me she found me attractive and she described some of my expressions which I didn't know I had. I checked in a mirror but couldn't reproduce any of them. I told her I found her attractive. We kissed long and slow. We discussed everything voraciously. We laughed hard. And then we laughed not so hard at her news that she was going travelling.

She'd always wanted to see the world and now a friend of hers had suggested they go together and she'd agreed.

'I also want to stay and see where this is going,' she told me. 'But I have to get something out of my system, and I'm not sure if I'm ready to dive straight back into another relationship.' She had been in a relationship since she was a teenager, and it had only recently ended. 'I want to see the world. You could come with me.'

'I can't.'

She nodded. 'You're already married. You're married to your career. That's why you find it so hard to find a permanent partner.'

I knew there was some truth in the statement. 'Call me when you get back. I might still be available.' We kissed some more, and I left her looking a pretty picture in the lambent candlelight.

Back at base I wrote emails all night. I wrote them without any enthusiasm. After my snowboarding accident, I climbed back onto my snowboard. This felt much the same. Emily had just caused a mission-crash.

Boldness doesn't genuflect to disappointment. It marches over it, blowing a trumpet. Forward and on. My wife was out there somewhere and I intended to find her. So I'd leap onto my white charger and go questing.

On one dating site, I found an exceptionally attractive Angela, so, knowing that women like to be told how attractive they are, I told her:

Angela, you have such big blue eyes that I found myself wanting to swim in them wearing flippers. Your hair is so long and bouncy that I fancied myself living in a tree house in a big brown forest that is long and bouncy. Your skin is so tanned that I had to turn the colour down on my computer screen in case an albino looked over my shoulder and cried. Your teeth are so perfect that I printed them off, cut them out, and am now wearing them as my teeth. Your eyebrows are like an artist's finishing touch and have obviously been created by a deft swish of his brush after which he had to leave the country for a year, visit his mother and cry, make a coffee, and finally burst back into his studio tripping over a bucket and take a deep breath before looking again at the picture and realising that it was everything he thought it was and that he could now retire.

Having said all that, don't go thinking you're too good for me! Fancy a date?

Carey

And I wrote to a Sandra:

Sandra, you have potential interestingality dripping off you in such large dollops that you are worth making up words for like interestingality. You also have enticementnocity, seductoriousness, and prettymustion. These are all qualities that I did not know I was looking for because who would know such a thing but that I have realised I am. I would like to take you on a date to a paper mill or somewhere interesting. You can choose between those options. Actually, how about a date in a shampoo-demonstrating laboratory? The excuse that you are washing your hair that day will not work in this instance. I think you would like me because I am romantient.

I jumped onto another dating site and sent a few messages. I found an Emma who had a very happy, smiley picture on her profile. I wrote,

Hello Emma, you seem cool from your profile but then again for all I know in the photo above you might be strangling a baby duck just out of eyeshot. I don't think you are strangling a baby duck 'cos there is no sign of that happening at all but now that the thought has occurred to me I just can't help seeing what I thought was a radiant smile as a malicious, sadistic baby duck-murdering grimace. Suddenly everything makes sense. In your profile, you mention beaches and water several times. You are obviously obsessed with ducks. I only wrote to you 'cos you seemed normal and now I'm thinking that you must be a bit crazy. Hold on, ducks are more likely to be found in lakes than on beaches... hmmm... I'm obviously wrong. You're not hunting and killing ducks are you? Sorry. It's obviously gulls that you're killing.

Anyway, I thought I would say hello and if you would like to say hello back then that would be a good starting point that could lead to other pleasantries. Soon, I'll be asking how your aunt's in-growing toenail is doing. If you really are a gull-killer, and I still suspect that you might be, then I would still like to get to know you so long as you at least try and quit.

Good choice of book – one of my all time favourites. Sometimes, when no one else is around, I like to pretend that I wrote it.

Her favourite book, according to her profile, is *Catch-22* by Joseph Heller.

I realised I was spending hours of my time writing nonsense to women. I should be doing something more productive, so I paced my room for a few hours, feeling unusual.

May wound up with three terrible dates.

Cassy the Fanatical Feminist

Cropped brown hair on a robust face that was devoid of movement or expression over a pugnacious lower jaw that did all the work when talking. She achieved a faint smile as we met, drew away when I moved to say hello and then stamped the nature of our date on the bar with a five-pound note and her opening words: 'I'll pay for the first round, you get the next one. We'll go halves on the meal.'

'Hello,' I said, offering a hand, which she shook almost with surprise, as though she hadn't expected human contact. 'My name's Carey.'

'Cassy,' she replied.

Over two drinks we discussed how marriage was only of benefit to men and is a tool men use to keep women subjugated. She was hardcore and oafish; she hijacked every conversation back to her favourite topic and seemed to be on her own mission: to emasculate the whole world by the end of our date.

Over dinner, she castigated me for using the term 'girls' when describing some of my female friends; she said I was de-powering women. I have no problem with feminists, but I've always found that the people I get on with best aren't black-and-white in their perception of words. All swear words, for example, are destined to become cute, or obsolete, or to alter their meaning. 'Bloody' caused people to leave the theatre when first used, in *Pygmalion* in 1914; today it's considered mild. 'Son of a gun' could today only be used humorously. My favourite swear word is that great British word 'bollocks'. 'Bollocks' becomes its own antonym simply by adding the definite article. If the show was 'bollocks', it was rubbish. If the show was 'the bollocks', it was great. Now attach those highly versatile testicles to a canine, and you can describe something as top-of-the-range: it was 'the dog's bollocks'. What a great word.

'Girl' is another great word when used right: not patronisingly or to indicate a lack of respect, but affectionately and – damnit, let's come clean – because endless repetition of 'women' becomes tedious and irritating. It's much easier to write about men because one has a choice of neutral words like man, bloke, chap, fellow, geezer, lad and so on; but where are the synonyms when it comes to women?

I had only moments earlier used 'boys' while talking about my male friends and this hadn't drawn from Cassy any accusations of de-powering men. Over 'girl', though, she was as inflexible as prison rules.

I think this kind of feminist gives a bad reputation to feminism and that therefore she is feminism's problem and not mine. But at the time I was still reeling from Cyclops's accusation of being unethical so I reacted apologetically to Cassy's argument and spent another hour watching her tongue shovelling drivel out of her mouth.

She did, however, confirm the lesson I'd learnt from my date with Bouncy. My wife would have to have a broader outlook.

Denise

Her brunette hair rose way above her head, as if the stylist had been engrossed in a surfing film while he worked, and her submerged face wore plunge earrings which matched her plunging figure. She was about ten years older than the photograph of herself she'd sent.

She'd told me on the phone that she loves steak so I took her to a steak house in central London. She'd also told me that she'd contacted my website after reading my *Writers' Forum* article – in it I'd given reasons why my ideal wife might be a writer.

'So what do you write?' I asked as I sawed into a steak that was as overdone as my date's make-up.

She confessed that she wasn't actually a writer; the magazine belonged to a friend of hers.

'No problem,' I said. 'My wife doesn't have to be a writer. It was just a good angle for the article and had some truth because I realised how influenced I've been this year by women's writing. I'm a sucker for a good letter.'

I didn't mind that she wasn't a writer. I did mind about the deception. I asked if there was anything else I should know about her. She assured me there wasn't. Yet at the end of the meal she told me she was married.

'Why did you come out on a date with me, then?' I asked – quite reasonably, I think.

'Don't get all crabby about it,' she said with peevish bemusement that she seemed to think I deserved. She explained that she just liked to go out on dates occasionally and her husband didn't mind.

'Didn't it occur to you that the person you're dating might mind?'

I stayed with her for another hour and discussed the matter as genially and ethically as I could. I'd paid for the meal and I paid for these extra drinks. I advised her, nicely, that she needed to stop her strange dating game, because people don't like being lied to and someone was bound to take serious offence.

I took my serious offence back home, where I seethed.

In the evening, I went off to a date which I really wanted to cancel. I wanted to cancel it because of fatigue and because I'd begun to lose all excitement in my mission. I didn't think I would ever find my wife this way, at least not with all the other pressures, and with having to be ethical all the time.

Stacey

I met her in the pub in London that had become my main meeting point. She was tall and attractive. She approached me and asked if I was Carey. I said I was. She slapped my face.

I actually let her aggression go, bought her a drink and tried to talk to her because I was so aware of trying to be ethical. When I asked why she'd slapped me, she said it was because she fancied me. She had a strange teenage-thing going with her attitude to fancying me. She displayed her interest with a lot of unnecessary, unamusing, and nasty insults. Then I snapped and thought, Sod being ethical and sod putting up with this bullshit. I told Stacey I'd be happy never to meet her ever again.

I had entered into this for an enjoyable experiment which would involve meeting nice people. The pressure of having to be ethical had become a burden that carried too much weight, especially while no one seemed to know what the hell being ethical actually meant. My career was about to fall apart because I had no time to commit to my Edinburgh show, I was failing to write a book, and I was missing my family and friends, whom I no longer had time to see.

I'd had enough. My wife-search was over. I declared my mission a failure and left the pub.

When I got home, I saw the air tickets for Prague on my bed where I'd left them and I thought about the lovely Jode.

End-of-May Report

May was wacky.

The loss of Emily was a major blow. But even if she'd decided to stay and we'd become serious it might still have been a mistake. She was fresh out of a twelve-year relationship and needed time for adjustment.

I'd been hoping things would kick off with her and I could slow or stop the dating and start writing a show and a book. But now I was back to having to make something happen.

At least I'd achieved one of the things on my list that would make me eligible. I'd quit smoking. The other items would have to wait until I came close to finding a wife and could cool off the dating.

So far, I hadn't met any of my dates near a restaurant in the chain that had offered me free chicken, but there was always a Chinese restaurant nearby, which was usually acceptable. By the end of May I'd had thirty Chinese meals on dates. I was beginning to get sick of

Chinese food, but still suggested it because suggesting it had become a habit.

In May, I performed twenty-one gigs in nine cities. I sometimes came straight back to a date and then went home to catch up with emails. My phone rang incessantly. I kept a comprehensive diary and wrote material for my Edinburgh show. Tiredness and stress had given me a batch of white hairs and made my skin pallid and drawn. The permanent bags under my eyes looked as if they could have held a week's shopping.

May brought me eight mini-dates and fourteen arranged dates (two of which were second dates). In total, I'd had dates with sixty-two women. On one of the mini-dates, a girl called Jacqueline had particularly stood out. She was a Nigerian girl who was mean at chess. She beat me several times. However, there was a mishap when I went back to the dressing room to get my things. While I was there, the club emptied and Jacqueline was thrown out with everyone else. I hadn't got her number.

I also had a mini-date with a girl called Holly who blew me away, but I thought my mission had blown her out because she seemed reticent when I told her about it. She did agree to another date, though, and I maintained contact to maintain her promise.

The interpretation of my mission had changed. The gossip paid no heed to my mission statement. Every time it came back to me I heard that I was trying to find a wife by the end of the Edinburgh Festival, by the end of August, and people voiced expectations that I'd fail and hopes that I'd succeed for my own sake, as if my happiness and reputation depended on it. I kept trying to steer the gossip back to the mission statement. I didn't want this extra pressure because I didn't want my task to become a competition. It was an experiment to be carried out for better or worse. But the gossip was not dirigible.

'Have you found a wife yet?' asked a girl called Melissa.

'No, not yet,' I told her.

'Oh, please find a wife. I want you to get married. We all want you to succeed.'

'I'm looking for true love, not just to get married for the hell of it. That would be easy.'

'Oh, please get married,' she repeated. 'It will be so cool if you manage it.'

I wasn't desperate to be married and didn't want my mission to become desperate. I wanted to be excited about it. I wanted to be excited about the possibility of a result. The thought that I might actually meet my ideal partner and marry her was tantalising. But I'd never said I believed it would happen or that I'd make it happen. Now, however, everyone else saw it as a personal challenge in which failure would be disastrous.

I'm normally quite controlled, but May had been a mood-swinging month that left me shattered. Cyclops's accusation had devastated the fun and made me very self-aware, which is why I spent so much time emailing. I did not want anyone to think I was using people. Selina the Devil had provided me with a momentous evening which raised me from the dumps and made everything rosy again. And then Emily's decision to travel and the last few dates made me fed up with whole damn thing. The chance of finding my ideal partner seemed bleak and this disappointed me because I felt I'd come close. My energy was sapped and burnt out from weariness. My mission had slumped into an imbroglio.

OhMyGodIt'sJune

I achieved a percentage tidy of my bedroom and went off to catch a plane to Prague. I was hungry, but decided to leave plenty of time to get to the airport so that I could have a meal and buy a present for Jode before my flight. The train to Stansted was cancelled and replaced by a bus service. The driver announced that we would be very delayed because the M11 had been closed and the traffic was terrible. I arrived at the airport with just enough time to jump on the plane. As I collapsed into my seat, stuffing a disgusting sandwich into my face, the pilot announced that the flight had been delayed by another half an hour and that I'd have had time to get something decent to eat and buy the present. He didn't actually say the last bit aloud, but he did in my head.

Jode

It was hot when I arrived in Prague. Jode met me at the airport and took me on trams and trains to her home. She was as sexy, relaxed, and good to be around as I remembered her. I knew straight away that this visit was a good decision. My quest might end right here in Prague. I could see myself marrying Jode.

Prague is a beautiful and romantic city. Every corner you turn brings new surprises of uneven alleyways with carvings and statues. The dramatic and often fairytale architecture boasts High Gothic, baroque, and art nouveau structures.

Jode showed me the astronomical clock and told me that when it was built, in the fifteenth century, the townspeople were so worried that the architect would create something equally amazing and beautiful elsewhere that they gouged his eyes out to make sure he couldn't. I'm sure there's a lesson in there somewhere but I'm not sure what it is.

The city is only fifteen years into experiencing freedom from Russia, and has a history of defenestrating its former rulers. Defenestrating people (throwing them out of a window) is not a very nice thing to do. Frequently the defenestrated people would land impaled on spikes. Despite being very nasty, there is something about it that is also funny, perhaps because the word 'defenestration' is funny and perhaps because the thought of throwing a ruling party out the window is funny. I'm sure there is a lesson in there somewhere, too.

The people of Prague largely eat fried cheese and goulash, both of which I tried but neither of which I fully appreciated.

Jode took Monday off work to spend time with me and show me around. She'd quit smoking a few months earlier and turned out to be the strength I needed to stay quit. She was happy for me to raise the subject of cigarettes and discuss it with me as often as I wished. We walked all over the city and finally found a quiet bar by the river, where we could sit outside and talk. A man came along the riverbank, stopped next to us and urinated into the water. A moment later, another man did the same. As a third man approached, Jode remarked, 'I think the romantic area we've chosen is the toilet.'

I'd hoped to get lots of work done on the Tuesday and Wednesday while she was at work, but she had the builders in. They marched into the bedroom every morning at seven o'clock and took over the place. I woke up and found that Jode had gone to work and there were builders standing around me in the bedroom and working in the bathroom, which meant I couldn't so much as have a wash, let alone get any work done, so I walked the streets until Jode returned from work.

I always enjoy spending time with Jode, but would she marry me?

At one point she said she had to make a difficult choice, between accepting a promotion she had been offered at work, and continuing her travels as she'd intended when she left Britain. Sometimes you can hear someone wavering about a decision that they don't know they've already made. I told her she should keep travelling.

That isn't the main reason we won't marry, though. We couldn't see eye to eye on whether pickled cabbage is a good thing. It is not.

Lesson

If it hadn't been for my wife search, it wouldn't have occurred to me to go to Prague and see Jode. Sure, I adored the time I'd spent with her at the Reading Festival but I'd have waited, on the off-chance that she'd return to England one day and look me up. For years I'd wallowed in a disappointing single life when I had quality women like Jode just two hours away. By trying to get married, I was learning how to be single.

On the day I arrived back in London, I looked in my diary, said, 'OhmyGodit'sJune,' and discovered that I had a date with a lady from *Grazia*, a new weekly women's glossy magazine. They'd requested that I wear summer clothing for the photos. I visited a fashion shop near my home and told a man called George about the shoot. He dressed me in high-fashion gear while keeping a commentary going about what is and isn't in. Apparently, pink is in for men, T-shirts are considered smarter than shirts, and very baggy trousers are a must. I'd never gone for the very baggy look, but I tried it and it seemed to work for me. I immediately understood why kids walk with that strange swaying motion — they're doing hoopla to keep their trousers up.

I was pleased that I'd made an attempt at another item on my list of things to achieve. Stop smoking — check. Dress better — check.

I left the shop with new clothes from head to foot and looking decidedly with-it. Next came the haircut. And then off for my date at a Gordon Ramsay restaurant in London.

Tanya

I was photographed to look as if I'd just arrived, and then photographed to look as if I was engrossed in conversation with Tanya, while in fact we were discussing how hard it is to look engrossed in conversation for a photo shoot. This conversation became quite engrossing. Eventually we were left alone to have our meal.

The slightly odd thing about this date was that we both knew that we were each intending to write about the other. I guess the difference was that I kept telling girls what I intended to write about them, and even asked their permission, whereas Tanya gave me no clues. She told me she had to report on such things as whether I made a good first impression, but she would not tell me if I had. I didn't know what kind of first impression I'd made; as soon as I walked in I'd been grabbed by the photographers.

It was a very pleasant evening, and Tanya was good company. She was a relaxed yet assertive professional girl who'd found a comfortable niche in a profession which seemed to suit her. I thoroughly enjoyed the evening.

I confessed that I hadn't entered into my mission for the most honourable of reasons. The initial idea had been for a show. I was sceptical about whether I'd really find a wife this way. She replied with something that grabbed my attention: 'They say it's the sceptics who find true love.'

I wasn't certain if this was a well-known phrase I'd never heard, but it made immediate sense and gave me a new purpose.

Lesson

Tanya's comment pleased me immensely because it gave my endeavour a new validity. When a sceptic has good news, it carries weight. If an incurable romantic who loves being in love for love's sake falls in love, it means little and makes most of us shake our heads and shrug. But if a sceptic can find true love, that means something. For the first time, I believed that I really was the right person to be getting all the attention I was receiving. I was doing something important. I could carry out my mission in a methodical manner and show the results to all intelligent people who cared. I wouldn't be dragged into the reality-TV style approach to the project. It wasn't a competition. It wasn't a game. It was an experiment.

And if that experiment resulted in true love, other people who have low expectations of ever escaping singledom would benefit from my experience.

If I were just trying to get married for a bet, on the other hand, then I would be merely that idiot who got married for a bet.

Filled with a new sense of purpose by the time I said goodnight to Tanya, I skipped all the way home. I'd become an authority on dating and had good news for everyone. Instead of complaining about the complications on the dating scene, I'd do something about it. I'd spread the word. People would lose their shyness and embarrassment, and everybody would have more fun because of me, and this would make my mission a sight easier. It was time for the sceptic to speak out about his findings so far. I had to stop skipping first, though, because no one takes a man seriously while he's skipping.

DATING SECRETS
WITH CAREY MARX

Dating is fun and it's easy. It goes wrong because people invest too much expectation in their night out or because – and I've found that this is the most common problem – they enter into it with the certainty that they'll be disappointed. I'm quite convinced that your attitude before the date is the biggest factor in deciding the date's success. If the attitude is right by both parties, it will take a lot of mishaps for the date to go wrong.

In calling a date 'successful', I don't mean that it will lead to sex that night or even to a lasting friendship. You're going out with a stranger or near-stranger: those goals are a lot to ask or expect. A successful date would be a fun night out which was worth going out for. Don't go on a date demanding any more than that and you'll be unlikely to return fretting over a waste of your time. Imagine, for example, that you and your date are halfway through a meal when your date gets attacked by a shark. If you left the house hoping for sex with this stranger, you'll be even more disappointed at seeing him/her being chomped by a large fish. Without a set agenda, you're more likely to relax and take the burden of perfection off the other person, and he or she will relax, too, which will make both of you less vulnerable to a shark attack (panic attracts sharks).

I've found this year that the people who complain about dating and those who are afraid of it have been over-influenced by whingeing, dissatisfied people who've got it all wrong. (Marriage, incidentally, gets a similar bad press because good news and fun dates bore cynics and gossip-spreaders.) Whingeing people never have fun because fun people avoid them.

Don't ask someone, 'Will you have a date with me?' unless you're fairly confident of the answer you'll get, because this question demands an immediate yes or no. I've found it best to say, 'I'd love to take you out on a date,' and let the person think about it. Normally, you get an answer immediately, but either way it's far less awkward. It's also good to suggest a specific date that you think that person might enjoy, or to use the old tried-and-tested ruse of saying you have two tickets for a particular show and ask if he or she would like to join you. Discussing where you might go for your date is all part of the fun and a good way to get to know this person and his or her likes and dislikes.

Don't be afraid of the word 'date'. There's nothing more awkward than a night out with someone when neither of you is sure if you're on a date or not. Those evenings rarely end in even a goodnight kiss. So use the word 'date' or say, 'I'd like to take you out' (everyone, male or female, likes the idea of being taken out for an evening). Don't say, 'Why don't we discuss our mutual business interest over dinner tomorrow?' That might be appropriate in some situations, or you might be able to imply that you want a date, but you'll still have to make yourself clear later. Much better to be honest from the word go.

Someone turning down your suggestion of a date shouldn't offend you or leave you feeling belittled. If it's done nastily, you clearly had that person's character all wrong, and you wouldn't and shouldn't want to date them. Remain calm, smile nicely, say 'I hope you get eaten by a shark,' and walk away. If the refusal is polite, you should have no complaint. We'd all like to be everyone else's type but we can't be, so it's no big deal.

Try not to interview your date on the date. You've decided to have a nice night out with this person, so don't then turn the date into a test to see if that person's going to be significant in your future. If you get on well, you will see him or her again. When you meet, discuss your day, the setting where you have met, his or her day, biscuits, shark attacks or anything other than 'What do you do for a living? How old are you? How much do you earn? How old are your parents? Do you like cats?' etc.

If you aren't good at talking to a total stranger, come armed. Buy a newspaper or magazine, find something in it that you have something to say about, turn up slightly early, be reading it when your date arrives, and start talking about it. Try not to choose something so esoteric that the other person won't know about or it will look as if you're showing off. Basically, find out about the person slowly and naturally during your date, not all at once, especially during the first fifteen minutes. If you really have to interview your date, at least don't bring out a notepad and pen and make notes of his or her answers.

I've already covered arriving late, so let's deal with another problem: forgetting your date's name. It's probably best to admit you've forgotten, but why do what's probably 'best' when there's almost always something even better? What you need is a ruse. Here's how I handled it when it happened to me.

Halfway through the meal we started talking about music and I mentioned that I only know of one song with my name in it, 'Carey Get out Your Cane' by Joni Mitchell. I asked the girl how many songs had her name in it. She named a few, and I added some. It all looked totally innocent and she had no clue that I'd forgotten her name — although she will have when she reads this.

OK, that ruse was a bit of a risk because there might not have been a song with her name in it. Here's another one, which always works and which I've used several times. Claim that you recently read an article on graphology, the study of character analysis from handwriting. You can say that you believe in it, or that you think it's rubbish, but it would be interesting to carry out a test. Get the person to write a short sentence and then to write their name in block capitals underneath followed by their signature. Then make up some bullshit.

It's easy. Just be logical. 'Small handwriting shows that you're conscientious and your careful dotting of *i*s and crossing of *t*s shows you like attention to detail. Your circular letters have gaps in the circles, which suggests you are quite open but this knotted *o* suggests that you're good at keeping a secret if you think it's necessary. You've written your surname bigger than your first name, which means that you put other people before yourself. The way you write your name in block capitals is how you present yourself to other people, and once again you're meticulous and your open letters show honesty. The signature represents the way you see yourself, and it displays a lot of sharp angles, suggesting that you're a thieving liar who's out to hurt people.'

Don't say that last bit. That was a mistake. Simply say complimentary things and the person you're talking to will usually be impressed. If they aren't, admit that you aren't, either. You'll both laugh about it, and you'll have found out the name by this brilliant device. You'll feel so impressed with yourself that you'll probably now have to admit you'd forgotten their name so that you can tell them how cleverly you found it out.

Incidentally, the bit about the writing showing that the writer is both open and good at keeping secrets is the kind of contradictory compliment that character-readers and fortune-tellers like to aim for. It means little and applies to most people.

My next piece of advice is on kissing. Always kiss your date and do it as early as possible unless you don't sense any mutual fancying going on. It's just a kiss; you won't get pregnant – and if you do you'll have a wonderfully unusual story to tell at parties, especially if you're a boy. A kiss tells you a lot about your compatibility with someone, it costs nothing and it's nice. Always kiss your date on the cheek when he or she arrives, as this sets the tone for a romantic night. Go for a proper kiss long before the goodbye, or you might make the goodbye awkward. Don't act like a shy teenager (unless you are a shy teenager).

If you haven't chosen a bad moment, and haven't done anything silly like leaping on your date over the dinner table, but he or she draws away, you'll have to assess whether it was a total mistake or not. It's worth risking that mistake on the off-chance that it won't be. If all goes well, the feel of the rest of the date will be much more comfortable. If all goes bad, assess whether you can still see that person for the rest of the evening as a friend or someone who wants to take things more slowly. So long as you weren't aggressive, don't apologise for wanting a kiss. Your date will have a hard time describing you as a monster on the grounds that you moved to kiss him or her while on what was supposed to be a romantic evening and after having a lot of fun.

Finally, we must deal with the embarrassment factor of dating. If you tell everyone that every time you go on a date it's a disaster and you're never going to meet someone, you'll fulfil your own prophecy. Have dates for fun and make them fun. Then tell everyone that you're having a great time going out on dates and they'll all want your life. It isn't embarrassing for a single person to be going out with other single people. If you're a lady and you think joining a dating agency is an admission of failure, you're wrong.

A very attractive girl I went out with told me she hadn't been asked out for three years. Another girl told me she prefers dating sites because she can get to know a man through emails before meeting him. Another gave me no reason except that she'd become addicted to the dating sites and loved spending hours writing to people. I'm not saying you must join a dating site. I'm using dating sites as an example of something that seems to embarrass many single people.

So unclasp your self-imposed shackles and start enjoying yourself. Let's work together to change the single scene into something more respect-worthy.

Oh, but don't go out on as many dates as I did; you will start to go insane.

Here are some other useful tips to guarantee a great date.

Don't surprise your date with zombies in a graveyard.

Don't surprise your date with zombies anywhere else.

Don't get drunk (unless you're a drunk, in which case do). People don't normally look attractive when throwing up. If your date does, arrange another evening out at once so that you can check whether he or she looks attractive when sober and not throwing up. You may have found one of the few people who look attractive only when throwing up.

Don't growl.

Don't go out with a dead person or you'll get strange looks, at the very least. There are no laws in Britain against dating dead people, but I don't think society is mature enough yet to handle such a scenario. Maybe one day people will grow up.

Don't be yourself (this rule applies to people who are unlikable).

Don't tell your date how many times he or she has said 'the fact that' and suggest using 'because' instead.

Do wear a name badge, and make it a large one. You should still introduce yourself as if you aren't wearing one, however. Have a name badge for your date ready and pin it on them.

Do wear a Superman outfit under your clothes and take a carrier bag with you. If your date turns out truly bad, put on a serious expression and announce, 'Someone, somewhere, needs my help.' Then strip down to the Superman outfit and run out of the door. Why the carrier bag? To put your outer clothes in so that you don't have to sneak sheepishly back into the restaurant a few minutes later to get them.

Do take shark-repellent spray with you. If you absolutely have to break any of these rules, don't let it be this one.

It felt incongruous that I was at last learning how to be single in the middle of a mission to escape my single life. Instead of finding my matching slipper, I was becoming really good at hopping.

On a break from dating, I met my friend Jo. She told me her thoughts on marriage (she'd been married for three years, I think). Jo's a fan of marriage. She advises friends who are in long-term relationships to get married because, she says, with marriage comes freedom. I hadn't heard it put that way before but I could see sense in it. A squatter might be wasting his time if he builds a new kitchen. Give him a piece of paper saying the house is his, and now all the work is for his own future and he can come and go without fear of losing it.

It was also interesting to see the marriage flag being flown so high by someone who isn't religious.

On arriving back in London, I decided to test my new skills at asking girls out on dates with a total stranger to prove what an expert I'd become.

I swapped carriages on the Underground a few times until I found an attractive girl sitting next to a man who was obviously annoying her because his elbow went over the armrest deep into her space. She asked him to remove his arm, and he complied with a look of contempt. She stood up and moved to another seat. I sat down next to her, wondering how to start the conversation. She was reading *Carrie*, a Stephen King novel. There was a thing or two I could say about *Carrie* because I'd seen the film, so I opened my mouth to volunteer my opinions – hoping I'd be able to change the subject swiftly before my two thoughts ran out. As I was about to speak, the oaf the girl had moved away from said, 'This is our stop,' and she jumped up to join him.

Soon, another girl sat down opposite me. She was mildly attractive. My brain stirred opening lines until it had jumbled them into a mush and then it unjumbled them into phrases she might use to tell me where to go. Why are we humans so bad at making conversation with strangers? We're so afraid of potential embarrassment. The biggest most embarrassing thing that can happen to us is embarrassment.

My mouth started to open but my brain panicked and closed it.

I didn't find another suitable candidate until I was on the bus approaching my home. The girl I chose was slim with very glossy long black hair which would have looked good in any shampoo commercial. Her eyes were a startling blue. She was reading Voltaire's *Candide*, which I have a number of things to say about, and this time I decided that I'd say them.

'Good book,' I said, nodding. 'Are you enjoying it?'

'I don't really get it,' she replied with a whine that her parents should have punished out of her years ago. She closed the book and dropped it into her bag, throwing me a look that told me she didn't wish to be educated on the book's merits. I gave up.

Holly

Holly had been one of last month's mini-dates and had dazzled me with her beauty and alluring charisma. I didn't expect her to agree to another date, however, because she felt a little uncomfortable with the public spectacle of my mission. She told me she understood and admired what I had set out to do, but didn't like the interpretation other people had put on it. She loathes reality TV programmes. I assured her that I wouldn't let my mission be dragged down into the sewers of cheap entertainment. It would remain honourable and dignified.

On our date in a Chinese restaurant in London, she told me she was proud to have been promoted from mini-date to proper date. I told her I was proud to have promoted her. We played a game of magnetic Scrabble, which I won by making up words and convincing her that they were real. It is one of my old magician habits. I also stole her watch three times.

Realising how compatible we were, we agreed to meet again, and I even considered cancelling all the other dates I'd planned. Holly told me not to, because she didn't want me to put that kind of pressure on her just yet. We set a date to meet again.

Her hair was gold, her voice was chocolate, her eyes were suns, her skin was electricity, her kiss emptied my brain.

I was falling in love at the drop of a hat. In my defence, I'd never seen so many women willing to drop 'em. Hats, that is.

Mia: Second Date

Mia is intelligent, clever, attractive and uniquely funny. Her emails exude character and normally start with something a little self-deprecating like this:

11/05/05

Today I realised how very optimistic I can be when I found myself getting into a lift in an unfamiliar building and randomly choosing the 6th floor in the hopes that it would deliver me to meeting room five, although I had been told earlier on that it was on the ground floor opposite the main entrance.

24/4/05

Today I realised how very understanding I can be when I allowed a man to stand on my foot for his entire tube journey, without once complaining to him, even though it was not at all crowded and there were plenty of places to sit down.

28/04/05

Today I realised how very magnanimous I can be when I allowed all three of my staff members to bunk off work with the excuse that they could not make it in because there was a rhino obstructing their only route into the office, even though they live in different parts of London and I had heard of no rhino-related incidents on the trains that morning.

Here's Mia on the subject of dating:

This week I had two occasions of gravitating toward men I had met online. The guy I met on Tuesday wasn't himself. In fact, he sent somebody else, who looked just enough like him for me to believe it was him, whilst all along thinking he looked completely different in his photo. It turned out okay in the end because I also sent a stand-in, who looks nothing like me. The guy I met on Thursday brought out the psychotherapist in me, although I tried hard to suppress it and encourage the pharmacist to emerge instead. Quite unexpectedly, the carpet-cleaner emerged in a dominant mood and it was all downhill from there. I will most likely see both of them again when I return to work in prisons.

For some reason, the word 'date' makes me want to make that face that people make when they've eaten something they think is a caper but aren't really sure what a caper is exactly. I think it sounds too official, requiring propriety, etiquette, a chaperone and musical accompaniment of Glenn Miller, which, although I enjoy, isn't the soundtrack I want to meet men to in my life right now. (Well, perhaps on Wednesdays). Instead of date, we could just agree to meet or get together or hook-up or assemble/congregate/liaise/connect/link-up/gravitate toward each other/muster, . . . then I'd feel a lot less uneasy.

Tell me when and where you want to see me, with sufficient advanced notice, and I'll be there, – possibly in a tutu, perhaps in a turban, no doubt, dressed inappropriately, but recognisable nonetheless.

We met in Islington wearing non-dance- or religion-based clothing and went to see a play called *Phallacy*. I think we both enjoyed the play and that we both had some criticisms of it. Mia remarked that it contained a lot of words. It did. After the play, we went for drinks until just about last Underground train time. We talked about the play and about life.

We kissed goodnight on the escalator in the Underground station and we were still kissing when we reached the bottom, so we fell over and landed in a way that would have been quite romantic on a hot, sandy beach with waves lapping up to our waists, but at the bottom of an escalator with people trying to step over us wasn't quite the same.

The next evening, I performed in Bow and had two mini-dates with very nice ladies, each of whom asked if she was my type. With each, I replied no. I was getting better at answering that question. In the past I'd have been afraid of insulting the person asking. It isn't an insult; it is a factual statement. I bought the drinks, just as I'd bought most of the meals for my dates. I'd so far spent around four thousand pounds on food and drink for my dates, and this didn't include money spent on entertainment that would make the taxman blanch.

It isn't necessary for the man to pay for a meal in this day and age. I did because these women agreed to be part of my show, or, rather, because I didn't want them to feel used. I paid for them because I was ethical. I've found that women, generally, still like it if the man pays, so long as it's done right. He shouldn't be forceful about it, especially because some women (though too few; far too few) will be offended by him paying. After all, a good date should feel romantic, and romance is rarely found in discussion over who had the prawn dish. I didn't mind that I'd been doing most of the paying, though I must point out an odd phenomenon: the least attractive and least likeable dates seemed to eat the biggest chunks of my wallet. (Caveat: there have been a few exceptions to that generalisation, so if you're reading this and I spent a lot of money on you that doesn't necessarily mean you're ugly and unlikeable). One thing that happened occasionally and did bother me was when the woman made no effort whatsoever even to reach for her purse or the bill, but simply waited for me to pay as if this was expected.

Jenni the Boatgirl came to my gig in Bow the next day. She had reluctantly let me pay for our meal the last time we met, though that was one of the occasions when paying was a pleasure. I spent some time with her and wished I could spend more, but I had to go home and write for my first full-length preview of the Edinburgh show the next day. We shared some lingering hugs which tested my resolve to leave. My resolve passed the test but my heart wasn't happy with it. This was willpower gone mad. I was on a quest for love, but had to keep abandoning my quest in order to do all the work involved in making it possible.

Among the emails from twelve new women, plus a number from women I'd dated recently, was one from Mia. When we'd parted company, she'd told me she'd like to see me again but that it might be an idea for me to contact her if I was still single after all this was over. In her latest email, however, she wrote:

> If you have time for another date with me before Edinburgh, choose the day and let me know as I would happily spend time in your wonderfully cynical company again, and might take you up on the offer to accompany you back home for a sing-along.
>
> I will marry the man who helps me overcome my fear of karaoke (assuming I don't kill him first).

She also suggested some alternative titles for my show:

1   *The Quest for the Perfect Wife Using Modern-day Methods for Meeting and Marrying*
2   *Everything You Ever Wanted to Know about Getting Married but Couldn't Be Bothered to Think About, Much Less Ask*
3   *The Art of Getting Married: A Single Man's Guide to Chaperone-less Courting and Cavorting*
4   *Going Down: How to Leave the Bottom of an Escalator Gracelessly Whilst Kissing a Near-stranger* (my personal favourite and best dating moment so far. I am prepared to re-enact it on video if you intend to use visual aids in your show)
5   *The Hows and Wows and Sacred Cows of Getting around to Marriage Vows*

I definitely wanted to see Mia again. Her self-deprecating façade was acceptable because it was masterful and I hadn't figured out yet if it was indeed a façade. There were a number of things about her that I hadn't sussed out. Yet, despite a certain amount of mystery, Mia was open in answering questions and seemed to have a generous view of the world around her. One thing was certain: she was a great date and while I couldn't predict where we were heading I knew that she would at the very least be a great new friend.

Various women kept me on the phone for four hours, after which I decided that there were now enough women in my life and I should stop seeing any more. Then I checked my diary and discovered I was late for another date.

I needed a secretary. One of the girls I'd dated had offered to take the job and then she typed a letter at a speed which would have made my mission last for six years. I told her I could type faster with my nipples.

My friend Janice came round and offered herself as my secretary and I employed her immediately. Her first job was to find me a romantic poem to learn, because learning a romantic poem was one of the things on my list to do to become eligible.

Emma II

Emma II was a different Emma from the Emma whose eyebrows are called Gin and Tonic. This Emma had been recommended by a friend. The friend had told her next to nothing about me, which left Emma a little surprised to find that she had walked into someone's show and book. She told me her friend had sent her the Edinburgh poster for my show but that she hadn't put two and two together. We went for a Chinese meal and got on OK, but there was no chemistry. Janice rang several times during the date and left romantic poems on my answering machine. The mood wasn't right for me to recite them.

Tracey, Anti-science Girl

She believed that all science was a lie. I thought she was joking and only slowly realised she wasn't. She didn't believe that rockets fly into outer space or that quantum physics is real.

'Do you believe in aeroplanes?' I asked.

'Yes, I know they exist, but that's not thanks to science. People just experimented with different shapes and engines until one worked. It's not science. Scientists are lying to us, claiming they did all this stuff.'

'Did the same happen with computers?'

She didn't answer the question. Instead, she started getting angry. 'I just don't believe anything I haven't seen with my own eyes.'

'Do you believe in history?'

'Yes. That's different.'

She wasn't a solipsist and had no respectable philosophy of her own or anyone else's to explain her bird-brained views.

We had differences of opinion on politics, food, money, science, religion, television, comedy, swearing, literature, social behaviour, morality, biscuits, and everything else. She received what I guessed to be a safety call from a friend and didn't seem grateful to science for this piece of security. Not my wife.

Lesson

I do not want a wife who is stupid.

MATE DATES

A couple of weeks earlier, my housemate Eva had suggested I ask one of our friends, Kirsty, out for a date. She suggested this in front of Kirsty. Kirsty had been one of the zombies in the cemetery. I'd only known her for a short while. We'd become friends very quickly but we didn't fancy each other, so a date seemed pointless. Then Kirsty said that she had never been taken out on a date so I thought that, seeing as I'd been spending a fortune on women, it would be nice to take a friend out, especially for her first ever date. So we agreed that we'd go out on a date, even though we absolutely knew that we wouldn't marry each other.

I trawled the internet for Sunday evening events (Kirsty would be giving music lessons during the day). I found nothing. There were helicopter rides and flying lessons, but not on Sunday evenings. I couldn't find any fairs or even a circus. No West End shows run on Sunday evenings. I tried many other avenues but they led nowhere.

On the train home from Cardiff on a boiling hot day came an announcement that a commuter had been hit by a train at a station further down the line. We were delayed for over an hour. The passenger next to me became very jumpy, kept looking at his watch and shouting at the driver's cabin to get going.

'I don't know what you're late for, mate,' I told him, 'but I'm missing a date with a top girl.'

'I just can't believe it's taking this long,' he ranted. 'I'm going to bang on the driver's door.'

'I wouldn't annoy them, mate,' I said. 'They've already killed one of us.'

Despite being late for my date, I felt quite relaxed. It was a date with a friend who'd forgive me for being late and had already told me I could write whatever I liked about her. This was all something of a relief compared to the complexities of all the other dates. I began to utterly get into the thought of this date.

Some time later, I dumped my stuff at home, showered, changed and trotted off into London to meet Kirsty.

We met at the pub that I'd used as a meeting point on many of the other dates. Kirsty had clearly come out in a great mood and ready to enjoy this, her first ever date. She has feisty, frizzy red hair which would easily win a fight against anyone else's hair even if the other person's hair had weapons. She has a laugh so infectious that her whole face catches it the moment it erupts.

We drank and I apologised for failing to come up with a Sunday-evening event. Kirsty cared not about events. The date was the event. 'I'm on a date,' she told me with glee. Her amusement became mine, too, and soon I was thinking, 'I'm on a date.' I'd been on so many dates that I'd become desensitised to the excitement of going out with a girl. But I woke up and remembered how much fun dating can be. I was having a night out with a really cool lady. What else would I rather be doing?

Kirsty suggested we ask everyone we meet where they thought we should eat. My camera had run out of battery, so we also decided to find people with cameras and see if any of them would take a picture and send it to us. This second idea was soon abandoned after we saw nobody with a camera. The first idea led to a number of suggestions, one of which was the Ivy, a somewhat classy and expensive restaurant. This seemed like a good idea so we strolled round there and were surprised that the doorman let me pass in jeans. We were told that a table could be saved for us at 10.30, so we went off pub-hopping until then. I hadn't eaten at all during this very hot day and got drunk very quickly.

The meal was excellent, and Kirsty coined the term 'mate date' for this type of date. I think it would be good to spread the word. There's a lot to be said for mate dates. Because we weren't trying to get off with each other, there was no agenda other than to have fun. There was no awkwardness in meeting, because we already knew each other, and we knew each other's sense of humour. Inasmuch as it is healthy to love your friends, such a date is still romantic because you're spending some one-on-one time with a friend and the evening is just for the two of you. I can recommend mate dates. Ask one of your friends out on a mate date immediately.

Kirsty suggested a game of dares, so I dared her to ask for a doggie-bag in this posh restaurant for the tiny morsel of duck she had left. She nearly asked – but didn't.

I asked what dare she'd have set me.

'I was going to dare you to steal the tablecloth,' she said.

Relieved that she hadn't, I went to the loo. I returned to find Kirsty with a doggie-bag in front of her and an expectant grin on her face.

When we arrived back at the house, Kirsty removed her coat and sat in the lounge with my housemates. I removed my coat and tablecloth and went to join them.

Because my housemates are Kirsty's friends I thought it would be funny if she had received a protection call from them. My housemates told me they'd actually been talking about making a protection call to both of us.

THE BIG CLEAROUT

My email accounts dribbled with guilt-impelling accusations, none of which were mean but all of which made me frustrated. I seemed to be spending a lot of time feeling guilty because I promised to call people and then failed and didn't easily find time to follow up these missed moments. I'd long since stopped contacting Becky, who was the very first girl I approached, and sadly I couldn't even remember what she looked like any more, which is probably why I no longer tried to contact her. I'd promised to see Karen (Phoenix) again for a proper date, but hadn't managed to contact her for several weeks. I didn't want to ring her at work during the day, and in the evenings I was too busy.

Sometimes I came home from dates and tried to phone women, but it wasn't good to call while I had drink in me, and even worse to explain to them that I was a bit tipsy because I'd got a bit drunk with another woman. Much of the time I found myself griping about all this, but really I felt constant guilt for being a big let-down. I wished I could shake this guilt, because then I'd be having such a great time.

The emailing had become a complex maze. An email I received might require as much as half an hour of research before I could reply. Say I had an email from a Wendy. I'd have to go through all my

195

emails and find the previous correspondence with that Wendy to see what she was referring to and be very careful that I was dealing with the right Wendy. Some of the emails were several pages long, so it could take a lot of rereading.

I had a filing system at first, but it had become a tortuous mess. One girl wrote, 'How is glasscow?' I searched through emails for hours to find out what on earth she or I had written about a glass cow and eventually left it as an unsolved puzzle. Days later, I tried again and realised that one of my emails to her mentioned being in Glasgow. She could not spell Glasgow and was under the impression I lived there.

I was in contact with around eighty women, many of whom wrote regularly; sometimes I spent all night writing responses. I realised that I was doing nothing to initiate new possibilities. I needed new. What I hoped to find was instant power-rapport. I would meet a woman and know she was The One. There were a handful of women who might become The One and I wasn't prepared to lose them but I had to cast the net out further to be certain I wasn't missing anything. If my mission didn't result in marriage, I wanted to show that I had at least been thorough.

My favourite women didn't babble my time away, and my wife wouldn't, either.

Lesson

My wife will not be a babbler.

It was time for a clearout. I wrote to many of the girls I'd been in contact with and some whom I'd dated and tentatively agreed another date with, and told them that I'd definitely not have time to see them again until I had announced my engagement, at which point I'd invite them to the wedding. I left on my list just girls with whom I had experienced some special spark, whether it had come from meeting them or from an exchange of emails that meant they might turn out to be the ideal partner I was looking for.

The book, the show and the mission had long ago conflated into one project in which each was integral to the others and yet each would have been surviving better without the others. I had to create more time to concentrate on likely candidates, though it felt unkind sending out emails to girls who'd become friends and girls I fancied (though not enough for a long-term relationship), to tell them that I wouldn't even be calling them for some time.

Have you ever felt bad about dumping someone? Try dumping sixty-five people in one night.

To my great relief, most of the replies were sympathetic. One was from Loki, who had been my very first date on my mission, although she was also an unwitting one because she hadn't been told about my wife-search. We'd certainly had a lot of fun, but we weren't heading for marriage. I mention her because her response to my email made me smile and was typical of her mature and admirable self-assured nature. She included a poem written by a Canadian poet whose name she couldn't remember:

> They laughed when they met
> And smiled when they parted
> And neither had time
> To be broken hearted . . .

Staring at my empty inbox was invigorating in a way that only a good rub-down with a pumice stone could compare to. I felt robust and purposeful, like good husband material.

The clearout had given me room to manoeuvre, and I began to feel organised. Back in the mood, I had a good feeling about my next date.

Next day I received an email from Becky, who was the very first girl I'd approached with this project, the girl who'd at first claimed to be a lesbian, and whom I had fallen out of contact with. I replied and told her how busy I'd been with all the dating. I think that put her off because she didn't write again.

I had a nice email from Meganetta, the giant. She'd been away. She'd also found a boyfriend.

Rhiannon rang. 'How's the mission going?' she asked.

'Feels like a learning curve that I took too fast.'

'Found anyone you want to marry yet?'

'I've met some fantastic women but I haven't fallen madly in love with any of them yet. I've fallen a bit in love with some of them. Is that enough reason to marry someone? Maybe I should just marry a joke candidate. It would be so easy.'

She asked me about my recent dates and I told her about Terry who was getting married and had attributed it to my mission.

'Me too,' said Rhiannon. She told me that as a result of a conversation on our date she'd contacted a man she'd fancied for years and told him she wanted to take him out on a date. 'One of my friends tried it too, though. She asked a man out and he said he didn't like women doing the asking.'

'I can't get my head round people like that. What world do they live in? I love it when a woman asks me out.'

'Anyway,' she continued, 'there's more. Our date led to a whirlwind romance that carried on for a week, and after a discussion that started with me telling him about your show he asked me to marry him. And I said yes.'

I told her I was very happy for her, which I was. 'I keep getting a feeling that my mission will end with everyone else married except me,' I said.

'That would be very funny,' she said.

I checked my mail on the dating sites and found I'd received a few flirts, but none from girls who would make me a good wife. One came from a nineteen-year-old who said she just wanted to have fun with an older man and she was certain I was that man. One was from a twenty-one-year-old who littered her email with exclamation marks, lols, and ha ha has, all in curiously odd places and who didn't seem to be able to write a logical sentence. The other flirts were from women whose requirements and views about life were mundane.

Tired and in need of a decent night's sleep I didn't reply to any of the flirts. I opened my email account just to see what needed doing – I had no intention of doing it immediately. When it opened, I was so shocked I actually stood up so that my jaw could drop as low as it needed to.

There were more new emails than ever. Along with all the emails from new women contacting me as a result of mentions in publications, on stage, and word of mouth, were emails from nearly all the women I'd written to during the Big Clearout. I scrolled through them, emitting sighs of disbelief. They wanted to know how things were going and if I was OK. I realised that I hadn't made it clear that I didn't have time even for common courtesy. The clearout had caused them all to write to me at once.

This was becoming an awful mess.

Next morning, I woke up late, spilt out of bed and rushed into London for a photo session and interview with the *Scotsman* newspaper. The photographer said he had a shot in mind involving me holding up some cufflinks. I couldn't imagine how cufflinks represented my show, but I nodded. We walked around Soho. I thought we were looking for a jewellery shop and was quite surprised when the photographer vanished into a sex shop and came out with some handcuffs. He thought handcuffs were called cufflinks. He also wanted me to don some rubber shorts. I assured him that he had my show all wrong and that it was supposed to be romantic. He didn't seem too convinced at first. Eventually, he photographed me with a rose sticking in one of my ears and apparently coming out the other. After the interview, I managed to get home for one hour, during which I did one hour of work, and then I sped off to a gig in Norwich.

Train Date

On my way to Norwich, I walked through the train and found an attractive woman sitting on her own.

'Is this seat free?' I asked.

'Yes,' she replied as she turned her head back to the window.

I knew that if I was going to get talking to her I should do it straight away because you can sometimes trick yourself into feeling confident but not after you've given yourself time to be certain that you aren't. She wasn't reading anything and I quickly found nothing about her suitable to bring up in conversation.

'It's a pleasure having this date with you,' I blurted. She faced me with a probing gaze. 'Oh, I'm sorry. Didn't you know this was a date?' I said. She smiled slightly. 'It's all the rage. Everyone's doing it. Surprise train dates. Don't tell me you didn't know.'

'Train dates,' she repeated, not giving me a clue as to whether I was getting anywhere.

Still riding on cheek, I had no choice but to continue. I pointed out some other unlikely pairs of people and suggested that they were all on train dates, including an elderly lady and a teenage girl. 'Mismatch,' I said. 'I'm Carey.' I offered my hand and she shook it.

'Janet,' she told me. 'Do you normally have *train dates?*'

'OK, you've got me. This is my first.' I looked down at the table in a got kind of way. 'Anyway, just because there's no such thing as train dates doesn't mean we shouldn't have one, does it?' This is a salesman trick. The 'does it?' followed by an instant smile and a look straight into the girl's eyes makes an answer imperative and a negative too uncomfortable for most people.

'No,' she said. Then for the first time she grinned and I knew I was amusing her. 'So how does a train date work?'

'I'm taking you out on a date on a train to wherever you're going anyway.'

'Does that mean you're going to pay for my ticket?'

'Oh, no. That's the beauty of train dates. It costs neither of us any more than we would have spent anyway on our journeys, and we get to tell people that we had a train date. If we get on well, we'll have to arrange to meet on another train. We should definitely get married on a train from London to Norwich. Perhaps we'll live on this train and build our lives around its route. Our children will go to school in Colchester; we'll do our shopping in Ipswich and party in Diss.'

We talked until her stop, which was Diss. Janet was a teacher in a junior school, a painter in her spare time, and a lover of science fiction books. She took my number before leaving the train, and before I reached Norwich I received a text from her saying that it had been her favourite train date and, thus, giving me her number.

A quick observation here about the text age we live in. The old 'Wait two days after meeting someone' rule is out the window. An amusing text straight after the date is acceptable and far better.

I didn't have a feeling that we'd meet again soon, although I did send her a text back. We'd agreed that she would come to my gig the next time I was in Norwich.

I'd managed to get a number from a total stranger on a train. I felt jubilant and empowered. This year had changed me. And I felt ready for the July that it had somehow become without fair warning.

End-of-June Report

In June I had eleven arranged dates and seven mini-dates. My total had reached eighty dates. The number of women I was in contact with by phone and email was over 110, despite the clearout. Mostly what the clearout had achieved is that the women who were waiting a long time for me to reply to them had become far more understanding. Their extra understanding made me feel guiltier for not replying.

On the mini-dates, which took place in various cities in and around gigs, I met an Amber who made shoes for a living and whom I liked enough to take out for lunch the next day, a Rachel who told me romance is dead, a Georgina who invents drinking games, a Jade who can do most accents effectively, and some other nice people. But none of these dates led to romance.

The mini-dates had been successful in that a few of my arranged dates had come from them, but generally they weren't as good as the arranged dates. They sometimes involved drunk women who'd seen me on stage and just thought what I was doing was funny, and sometimes involved women I didn't fancy at all but was too embarrassed to turn away after having announced my search on stage. My ability to turn people away had improved, but not enough for every situation.

Emily and I met for a last time before she left to travel the world. She was very excited about her travels, but she also cried when we said goodbye. We definitely had a nice thing going and we talked about holding out for each other. But this simply wouldn't have worked. She needed the break from her long relationship to re-establish her identity and, well, it's hard to put on paper without getting personal but she needed to be free for a while. We'll meet again, though.

Holly rang to tell me she was pregnant and that it was definitely mine. I said that in that case I would have no choice but to dump her. She couldn't have really been pregnant from me because we hadn't had sex. I was enamoured of Holly but somehow didn't think we would get married. I didn't know why I thought that, because everything about her delighted me.

Mia I loved, but I wasn't sure if it was relationship love. I also loved the company of Jenni the Boatgirl and it felt like relationship love but not necessarily life-commitment love. She communicated on my level, and we got on well and enjoyed each other's company, but she balked at the suggestion of marriage. I had a feeling that a relationship with Jenni would have to develop in its own natural way and would be destroyed by forcing my rushed mission upon it. I had so far only had one date with her and then seen her briefly again at a comedy club.

Basically, there was no sure thing happening. I would see Holly, Mia and Jenni again, and also see if any of the new dates I had planned would send my head spinning.

I'd tried not drinking on a couple of dates, but this proved unpopular. The girl would not drink, either, and the date had a stiffer quality. Whether they employ alcohol, caffeine or other substances, it seems that humans prefer a drug to enhance their socialising. I expect that if I hadn't been writing a show about all this, not drinking would have been more acceptable to me, but I felt a duty to these women to follow their lead in such matters and make them feel comfortable. Though I suggested many alternative meeting places and date ideas, most of the women wanted to meet in a pub and then go on for a meal.

Close to my home, I'd found a place offering martial arts courses on Monday evenings, but I had no Monday evenings free in my diary. In fact, I had no regular evenings or daytimes free, so I decided to leave 'Take fighting lessons to protect my wife' until I was up in Edinburgh when I'd be in one place for the month. Mostly I existed on an average three hours' sleep a night and had no time and little energy to 'Get fit'. My life had become a wife-hunt monomania and I couldn't remember what life had been like in the old days. I hadn't read a book all year.

Instead of becoming more eligible, I'd become less fit, more fat and stupider than I had ever been.

The battle against public misunderstanding of my mission had largely been lost. People weren't excited by my intelligent experiment approach. They wanted me to be carrying out a do-or-die attempt to find a wife by the end of August. I'd given up trying to re-educate them and had begun to accept the challenge they needed from me, though in essence I didn't like it. In a hotel room I watched an American programme in which men wearing coloured masks got to live in a house with a woman who rejected them one at a time. I hated it. I resolved that my show would not become a game show, yet the mission itself had. I heard it described as a competition and myself described as the prize. I didn't want to be a prize.

The non-experiment challenge to find a wife by the end of August was also more popular with the press, and I was getting a fair degree of press attention. Swimming with the powerful tide, I altered my mindset and took on the challenge.

I knuckled under and, instead of arguing with anyone's assertion that I was on a personal challenge that had to succeed or else it was all a waste of time, I started nodding, and then I started agreeing, and then I started announcing that I would find a wife by the end of the Festival. I had less than two months to achieve it.

THE JULY THAT CAME
WITHOUT FAIR WARNING

I couldn't fathom where my year had gone, let alone what had happened to June, which I was only just getting into. I took on a director called David for my show and told him that I was in big trouble and he had one month to sort it out. We spent an afternoon discussing the presentation. He had many good ideas and interesting points to make.

David suggested that one of the reasons why my quest appealed to so many people is that love is one consistency in a world of changing values. As people turn less to God for their sense of belonging, perhaps the quest for love becomes more poignant.

I was about to agree with him when there was a fierce thunderclap followed by a violent cloudburst, so I steered the subject away from God.

Keeping fit is easy but getting fit is hard, so I decided that it was time to do some fitness-getting. I went for a jog in the park with Phil and asked him to take me out every day until the Festival. I did some pull-ups (I was up to fourteen consecutive ups plus a few negatives), using the bar above my door, and I then did some hanging-upside-down exercises from the same bar.

Dress better – check. Stop smoking – check. Get fit – check.

Holly: Second Date

We met in west London, near her home. She wore a cross-over Chinese-style green top with a long black skirt, and looked so adorable and sensual that her beautiful smile became overload and disrobed me of confidence. I demonstrated my feeling of inadequacy during our meal by telling her at length about the tasks I'd set myself that would make me as eligible as possible and how I intended to complete them all during the Edinburgh Festival, when I'd have more time. I was trying to sell her the me that I could be.

She told me she liked me as I was.

She gave me one of her magical kisses that make my brain vanish.

Then she sat back, all scrumptious and heavenly.

We were in a classy restaurant which only employed waiters with stiff backs.

'Do you think you might marry me?' I asked, as she deftly put down her fork with her delectable fingers while I thought, 'I've never seen a girl put down a fork so beautifully.'

She blinked her seductive eyes and leant forward to whisper, 'I might.'

We both giggled for a bit. I looked out the window and watched clouds drifting dreamily across the sky. One of them looked vaguely heart-shaped and I pointed it out to Holly. 'A sign,' I said.

'I thought you didn't believe in that kind of thing?'

'Do you believe in it?' I asked, grinning stupidly, bewitched by her merciless beauty.

'Yes.'

'So do I.'

'I don't really.'

'Neither do I.'

A waiter bent to take our plates, folding as if his waist were a hinge, and keeping the stiffness of his back in check. He asked if sir and madam would like more wine and I asked for champagne. 'We're getting married,' I told him.

'Congratulations, sir.' He didn't seem particularly impressed. I wondered if he saw people winning impossible challenges all the time.

After the meal, we bought some wine and went to her house, where we sat in the lounge, played her guitars and sang at the tops of our not very melodious voices for many hours. As the night came on we moved into her garden and lay on our backs on the grass, staring up at the stars while we discussed absolutely everything in the world that could ever be discussed.

Lesson

Housemate Nick has a thing he does where he stands very stiff, holding onto the back of a chair, and announces that he is not feeling stressed. Then he walks off, holding the chair. It's very silly. I like silly jokes. Here is one I wrote: 'I bought a book of baby-names but I had to take it back and complain. It was full of adult names.'

Silly walks a funny-walk along a fine line and can sometimes fall off that line into facetious or stupid. But it's worth the risk. One of my favourite characteristics of Holly was that she could get really silly with me. I would like my wife to have that trait. I would like to be able to get drunk and sing songs and joke with my wife. If she isn't silly enough, she won't be able to put up with my guitar-playing or the songs I write, which are all extremely silly.

The downside of silly is that it's hard to tell when serious pops up. Holly agreed to marry me by the end of the Festival, but were we were both still being silly? Or did she mean it?

With Phil's encouragement, I kept up my new exercise programme for three days until he sprained his ankle by stepping into a hole in a field. I was a bit relieved, because the jogging was making me too tired for all the gigging, meetings, writing and dating.

I met director David. We thrashed out a number of hitches with the show. I told him that when reading through profiles of women on dating sites I didn't have a clear idea of characteristics that I was looking for, but I did have a clear idea of characteristics that put me off. He told me of an experiment he tried some time ago when he was single and on a dating site. The experiment was to see if a very simple advert that contained no characteristics to put people off would be a winner. He tried several versions, and the most successful was one which simply stated, 'Girl seeking man'. It received thirty replies straight away.

I told him that if I had tried an experiment that involved a dishonest advert, I'd have been accused of unethical behaviour.

Mia: Third Date

Mia had invited me to see *A Winter's Tale* at the Globe with her on Tuesday, 12 July. I liked the way she came up with date ideas that she booked.

I was flustered when I met her outside the theatre and she remarked on it. I'd spent the day sorting urgent requirements for the flyers and posters for my show, and having an interview with a reporter and another meeting with David. I'd written some things that needed writing and phoned some people who needed phoning, but I hadn't given a spare minute to someone who really needed it (me). I'd been on the phone all afternoon, all the way to our meeting and as I said hello to Mia.

'Which entrance is it?' I asked as I switched the phone off.

'I think it's this one,' she said.

'I thought you'd know. You're a scientist. How much were the tickets?'

'Don't worry. I'm paying. It's only five pounds to stand.'

'How long do we have to stand?'

'I don't know.'

'But you're a scientist!'

'Are you going to keep telling me that I'm a scientist?'

'Well, you are. You should know that being a ...'

'Scientist?'

'Exactly.'

'Anyway, they said on the phone that it's best to experience the Globe as a groundling.'

'What's a groundling?'

'Someone who stands.'

'I knew you'd know that. You scientists.'

'Are you going to be like this all night?'

Mia is such good company. She's calm, collected and thoughtful. She talks at an even pace. I amuse myself with the thought that she's hiding an outrageous temper which can smash all the contents of a house in minutes. There was, however, no sign of this.

A night at the Globe gets my recommendation. It took a few

minutes for my brain to adjust to Shakespearean language, and certainly this play is known for peculiar complexity and obscurity of language. One argument goes that obscurity was highly respected in Shakespeare's time; I guess people thought that if they couldn't understand it, it must be clever. The play has a number of credibility-holes in it that might have been acceptable in the sixteenth century and may have offended my need for explanation, but the entertainment value made those weaknesses feel like a good type of daft and I giggled, laughed and applauded throughout the three-hour performance. The last play I saw with Mia had too many words; this play had far more words than that one, and yet it never felt gratuitous. Mia pointed to one of the actresses on stage in her hoop skirt and said, 'I think that makes her bum look big.'

Despite enjoying the play, however, my evening was ruined because the Globe ran out of ice-cream during the interval and I was absolutely set on having one.

After the show, we wandered over the Millennium Bridge to find food and drink. When it came to dessert, I ordered an ice-cream. The waitress told me that the restaurant was closing soon a nd they'd locked the freezer. I will never go to that restaurant again as long as I live or allow any children that I ever have to use it, either.

We missed the last Underground trains and wandered into Trafalgar Square for buses. At one point, I heard Mia curse, looked over my shoulder and caught a weenie flash of anger. I thought she might be upset with me because of the long walk and because we hadn't stayed south of the river, which would have made it easier for her to get home. I believed I'd glimpsed the hidden rage that she must be keeping constantly at bay for fear that she would destroy the contents of a house in minutes. But it turned out that she was just cursing her shoes because they weren't comfortable for long walks.

On the way home, I managed to find myself an ice-cream and I rang Mia to show off.

The morning of Wednesday, 13 July leapt through a gap in my broken curtains and tore me out of bed, whispering commitments in my ear like a demonic Canadian, and then I realised it was just Phil, who is Canadian, whispering things in my ear while wearing a red shirt. He was telling me we were going out for lunch. I told him not to hide behind my curtain. We had lunch and I moaned about not having time to be eating with him and then I went home and moaned to some women about not having enough time to be moaning to them and rang David and moaned that I had no time to work on the show. Then I rang a few friends whom I had not moaned to for a while and I moaned to them, too. One friend suggested I stop the dating; one suggested I cancel the show; one suggested I ditch the book; another suggested I become thoroughly unethical and ignore all the women.

Phil said, 'You've come this far. See it through. You're on the last stretch. Push yourself until you can't take any more and then take some more. Collapse when it's over.'

'Is that your advice?' I asked.

'No. Craig said it to me when I was moaning about my sprained ankle.'

Our friend Craig is a larger-than-life character. He climbs, he snowboards, he white-water rafts. When Phil and I shared a house with him a few years ago, he built a climbing rope in our hallway; he had two punching bags in his room, one of which he knocked the stuffing out of; he bought gravity boots so he could hang upside down in the doorway to the hall, and was planning to turn all our walls into climbing walls so that he could get around the house without touching the floor, when we had to move out. In Oxford Street, he stopped a mugging by wrestling the mugger to the floor. He has a great-aunt who was the first woman to climb the Matterhorn.

'But Craig's the kind of guy who'd break both his legs just to make a jog up a mountain more difficult,' I said.

Phil had his own show and two plays to prepare for Edinburgh while nursing a sprained ankle. We both decided to take Craig's advice.

Jenni the Boatgirl: Third Date

We found a bar and a quiet corner. She asked how the dating was going and I told her a few highlights. It was a little embarrassing telling my dates about the other dates, and no matter how much some of them assured me that they wouldn't be bothered by the information they usually were a little, especially if I mentioned some of my favourite characteristics of the women I had met. Several asked if they were my favourite. Answering that question had to be avoided at all costs with the majority of them.

Jenni, on the other hand, is a down-to-earth realist, who happily handled my recounting of the dates and told me of dates she'd been on. She'd brought me a box of presents and made it very clear that the background of this present-buying had been that she'd been a bit down and wanted to buy things. So she bought some things for me; it was not a gesture of any more import than that. I was amused by her caveat-explanation.

In the box were individually wrapped items she'd bought with my busy schedule in mind: some caffeine tablets, some Echinacea tablets, a jar of pickled onions (I'd mentioned that I liked them), a plastic thing consisting of a stick and three hands which, when shaken, make a plastic-hand applause noise, a wind-up mobile-phone charger (which, unfortunately, didn't work for my phone), a small bottle of Blue Nun, and a book called *He and She*, which was first published in 1958 and gives boys advice about girls. We had a lot of mileage out of this book, which had chapters on understanding girls, making friends with them, morality and marriage.

We talked for hours. Jenni has natural. She does not have airs, graces and pretences. She is without effort. She is neither pastel nor flashy, neither common nor posh. Yet she has elegance, grace and savoir-faire. She is fantastic company.

We had agreed to go our separate ways by last Underground train times and I kept my drinking to a couple of pints, because I wanted to be sober enough to come home and write. But I was enjoying Jenni, so I had one more drink than I had intended. Then I had the idea that we should buy a small bottle of champagne and sit in a park and drink it until last Underground train times. It was the kind of idea that makes sense to someone who's just had one more drink than intended.

When we found champagne it was only in decent-sized bottles, but the endeavour had become a mission so I bought one. The park nearby was closed, so we sat by the Thames on a bench and pretended to be winos as we swigged from the bottle, and became quite intimate winos just as some friends of mine were walking past. We had a drunkenly wonderful night.

Lesson

Jenni's someone I wholly relax with. I don't have to do things other people would do to impress her. Many people want you to do what other people would do. I'm very likely to forget people's birthdays. Some people think I should remember their birthdays. That's because they want me to do what other people would do. One date said she thought I should have worn a suit for our date. That is something someone else would do. I want a girl who likes me to do what I would do.

I had three potential wives and many more back ups pouring in as a result of press coverage.

Marry Me had accumulated copious press interest. Freelance journalists contacted me, asking to write articles about my mission, and two television companies had shown interest. In January, this would have been exactly what I wanted. In July, however, I no longer had time to follow up these contacts efficiently. I kept arranging to meet one TV company and kept cancelling.

Looking back, I can see that I also suffered a lack of enthusiasm over letting my mission get any bigger. A company wanted to film me going out on dates but I'd learnt during the year that this would turn the dates into something unpleasant or even impossible. I'd encountered so much fear of the book and the show when approaching women that I couldn't imagine how few would date me if there were television cameras present, and I'd probably lose some of my most promising potentials. Since Cyclops I'd become aware of the detrimental effect that cameras can have on romance, even with the best intentions. I'd needed to develop better powers of reassurance to come this far, and that reassurance had often been too delicate to survive any greater threat of public interference.

Publications had a subtler effect that I could handle. So far, I had spoken on the phone to or had face to face interviews with reporters from the *Sunday Times*, *The Times*, the *Sunday Mail*, the *Mail*, the *Sun*, *Woman's Own*, *Grazia*, the *Scotsman*, and the *Fest*. I had written an article for *Writers' Forum*, the first article I'd ever written and, therefore, that I'd had published. My *Marry Me* soundbite show-title was doing its thing as it was supposed to. It opened doors for me, but I no longer had time to be going through doorways. The mission had outgrown my initial intentions for it.

I arrived in a restaurant in Islington for an interview with a lady called Louise from the *Sunday Times*. This was to be a group

interview. Louise sat with myself and two other acts who were going
to Edinburgh. She explained that she was going to ask questions and
that she wanted us to answer one at a time. Then she told us that the
angle of the piece was that we three men were all failures.

We pointed out jointly that none of us saw himself as a failure.

She held up the write-up of my show that I had penned without
much thought some months back in the inchoate days of my mission.
'But you're thirty-nine and you've failed to find a wife,' she pointed
out.

'Yes,' I said, 'but that doesn't make me a failure. I wasn't trying to
find a wife before this. I've also failed to go to Scunthorpe because I
have never had reason to go there.'

She was a very nice lady, who was clearly amused by our responses
to her angle. The interview turned out to be fun.

During an interview with a lady from *Woman's Own* I said I was
planning to work through a list of things to become more eligible.
One of those things was to buy a new fashionable wardrobe of clothes.
I'd so far been to a fashion shop and spent two hundred and
something pounds (for the *Grazia* shoot) on a fashionable look and
intended to spend a mound more with the help of a fashion guru
friend of mine. When the article came out, it read: 'I've given up
smoking and have just spent £200 on some trendier clothes to improve
my image. The reason is straightforward – I'm trying to find a wife.'
The inference is a little different, and friends who read it said it made
me look a right chav.

Despite that, I was grateful for the article because I'd really
wanted to get into *Woman's Own*. I was having a year of intense
female attention and to be infiltrating their magazines just felt right. I
never knew that getting into *Woman's Own* was an ambition of mine,
but it must have been because I was quite chuffed about it.

I received ten emails within three days of the article appearing

and they continued to come in from all over the country. An eighteen-
year-old girl in Liverpool told me that we were made for each other; a
forty-nine-year-old woman in Lancashire said the same thing. One
woman was desperate to get married. Another was against marriage
but said that she wanted to marry me anyway.

Tanya from *Grazia* had written a nice and complimentary article
about me. It also had a few lines that could not have amused my
friends more if she'd been playing to them in the first place.

> Carey looks nothing like his rubber-faced publicity shots. The
> funnyman scrubs up seriously well ... He is on time, thoughtful,
> articulate and laid-back, but his real plus point is his blend of
> energy, charisma, and schoolboyish charm ... But the biggest
> surprise is that Carey is a fantastic listener. I feel fascinating. If he
> were 6ft 2in, nut-brown, wearing a suit and a lot more goo in his
> hair, he'd clean up on the escort circuit.

One of my friends translated. 'She's saying that if you were better
looking you could be a prostitute.'

I was amused, but more than happy to accept Tanya's compliment.
I liked her and she'd given me new direction and a sense to my
mission at a time when I'd got a bit lost.

On the way to a preview in Shepherd's Bush, I sat on the
Underground train and put three publications that I'd finished with
on the seat next to me. The first was *Grazia*, which carried the full-
page article about me, with photos, in which Tanya had recommended
me as a date. The second was *Woman's Own* with its full-page article
and photo of me. The third was *Metro*, which had a particularly
complimentary article about my show. At the next stop, three women
got on the train together. One was a petite, punky girl with spiky hair
and her own fashion sense that worked. One was a tall, blonde, leggy

lady. The other was a lady in her late thirties, wearing a business suit and looking very sophisticated. All three were exceptionally attractive. One picked up *Woman's Own* and started to read it. One picked up *Metro* and started to read it. The other picked up *Grazia* and started to read it. I watched them flicking through their magazines and deeply regretted having just ripped out my pages from all three publications.

Nutter Moments

Every interviewer asked me about the nutters I'd met. Mostly I ducked the question and said I didn't want to give that impression of dating, because it hadn't been the bulk of my experience and it seemed too predictable an image. Sometimes I gave them just one incident.

Although I hadn't met many proper nutters on my dates, possibly because I'd been writing to most of them before our meeting and had chosen carefully, there had been a number of nutter moments. The problem with nutter moments is that you can't tell if the person responsible for that moment is a nutter or if they're just having a moment caused by a stressful day or whatever. Because of the nature of my project and my awareness of the power I had to write about people, I tried to be responsible and not compromise anyone's privacy by naming and shaming them for an odd habit or for behaviour that would humiliate them. But there were a few nutter moments and some absolute nutters who deserve name-free mentions.

Nutter one was terrified that I'd mention her in the book in any form, because her friend would find out that she was dating again so soon since after her last relationship, which had split up over two years ago.

Nutter two nearly threw a fit when I picked up a guitar in her room and started to strum it. I hadn't had much chance to practise for a few months, and it was good to have an opportunity to have a gentle strum whilst we were talking. She had a *thing* about people playing guitars in social situations. I found this weird and said that I'd leave if she wished or I'd put the guitar down if she could give me a reason. She said that I'd been looking in the mirror and pulling faces while playing. I said that I'd never done such a thing and that I found her attitude most confusing – I'd rather leave than put the guitar down and pretend that nothing a bit weird had happened. The moment passed but remains without explanation, although I am certain that it was a nutter moment and not a nutter, because I know her well now.

Nutter three collects matchboxes. She begged me not to mention in my book that she collects matchboxes. I was amused because I thought she was joking until the subject came up for around the twentieth time, by which point she was trying to get me to make this promise in writing.

Nutter four told me off for being friendly with a waitress. I wasn't being over-friendly, and certainly not sexual, just friendly. I can only imagine that this nutter had lost all her former boyfriends to waitresses.

During a mini-date at a comedy club, nutter five started crying about something her father said to her when she was twelve. He'd made fun of her for a poem she had written. By the end of the story she was bawling.

Nutter six. Just for a bit of fun to amuse myself, I decided to test the art of mirroring. The theory goes that when a couple are in harmony they drink, sit back, lean forward and eat in time with each other and you can give someone the feeling of harmony by deliberately copying them. I mirrored the girl easily and I thought quite effectively until she quite unashamedly and quite thoroughly picked her nose.

Nutter seven, who'd been acting quite ladylike and delicate, put down her handbag and announced, 'I'm just going for a shit.' Women tend to spend some time doing their make-up and hair and prettying themselves up, and it's unusual for them to use such an expression on a first date with someone they're trying to impress. I thought she was obviously not trying to impress me, but when she came back she said she fancied me and wanted to go on somewhere. This one doesn't really count as nutter or nutter moment, and I couldn't decide whether or not I respected and admired her blatancy.

Nutter eight had a mini-argument with me because she felt that I hadn't shown enough interest in her. She was referring to the infrequency of my replies to all her emails prior to our date. I ended up having to take her to an internet café and show her how full my email accounts were, before the argument ended.

Nutter nine was a recommended blind date. She spent most of the evening muttering. I did at one point tell her as politely as I could that she was muttering. I have no idea what she answered. Eventually I had to make excuses to leave, because I didn't know if we were having a conversation.

Nutter ten was, more and more often as time passed, Carey Marx. An example that springs to mind is when I accidentally called Holly 'Holly', and then had to explain it was her pseudonym in this book. Another was when I embarked on a mission to find a wife by the end of August.

Dates set up by friends can be surprisingly or disturbingly revealing about what type of person your friends think you might be compatible with.

One such date moaned, 'Dates are hard work . . . You just meet lots of idiots . . . Men just want to get you in bed . . . Men insist on paying for the meal . . . Men don't pay for the meal any more . . . You feel like you're being quizzed,' etc. She contradicted herself many times.

People who go out of the house with this attitude almost always return home having confirmed they were correct.

Backstage

'There's no business like show business' – thus goes the song, and I guess it may be true, but if there were any other business like show business it would probably be called 'show business' so it would be hard to tell.

In a café in Leicester Square, director David and I worked our way through a pile of notes, crossing things out, moving things, adding things and shrugging at things. David's eyes light up or dim as ideas strike him as good or fail to move him. I can throw a question his way and he'll react with a winning poker face for a full minute and then there's a flash smile as he finds an answer. We needed answers and we needed plenty of them. We poured our answers onto the table and found that each came with new questions.

'We've had five preview shows,' I said, 'and the reactions have been conflicting.'

David nodded thoughtfully.

The first preview had gone well but lasted over two hours. Since then we'd cut the show down to the hour it would have to be, but we'd lost too much vital information.

The emails and dating stories I could mention were ever changing as girls came and went from the project.

One presentation facet that I was dealing with was quite new to me. I felt responsible for the girls I mentioned. I only read out emails if I had the writer's permission, and all the ones I read were from women who were now friends of mine, but how the audience reacted to the emails and even to mentions of these women was of paramount importance. A comedian's natural instinct is to make fun of everything, but I had to use caution. If I read a piece of, say, Mia at a

preview and the audience didn't laugh with her and like her, I felt I'd
let her down and I lost some respect for the audience. I'd become
protective of my new friends, and resented talking about them to
audiences who did not get them.

Mostly, I named no more than a handful of women in the show,
and audience members told me it was too difficult trying to remember
who was who. I thought of adding more just to show them my pain.

Talking about dates was difficult. If I just related funny things
that I'd said or done on a date, it looked like showing off and gave the
impression that I was out on these dates as Mr Comedian. If I related
funny things the girls said or did, I'd be accused of getting laughs out
of other people's funnies. Most shared moments of humour on the
dates didn't come across at all because you had to be there.

If I was too nice about the women, the audience wanted the dirt.
If I gave them dirt, I felt filthy.

During or after a preview audience members discussed the
mission with me. There was an overwhelming consensus that I'd
behaved well and hadn't been unethical, which had been one of my
concerns. Women were very supportive over my methods and
approach. People discussed dating and romance with me. Many asked
if I had sex with any of the women. One man saved me from the
question one night by saying, 'He's had eighty-five dates. If he hadn't
had sex with any of them, that would be a pretty poor hit rate.' Most
audiences were mature enough for me to answer the question
honestly.

After one preview I had three complaints. I also had a mini-date
with a girl from the audience called Mandy. She was laid-back, cool,
funny and confident. We went for a meal after the gig. She told me
she loved the show.

'I don't understand the complaints,' I told her. 'I wasn't confessing
anything evil.'

She laughed. 'The first man who complained was upset because of his religious convictions,' she explained. 'He wore a cross on a chain round his neck and one on his wrist. The woman who complained was sitting near me. I saw her reacting wrong all over the place. She tutted when you mentioned sex, without listening to what you were saying.'

I'd shared truth with the audience. The mission had started as a load of frolicking fun. From an empty love life I jumped into a pool of women and found myself swimming in girls afraid to do the breaststroke. It built to the most fun I'd had for years, and for a short time back there it was the honeymoon before the wedding. Then there had been a build in the numbers, romantic disappointments and so much hard work. I'd been forced to become more businesslike.

'The other guy who complained,' said Mandy, 'was jealous. It was all over his face.'

'Maybe I shouldn't mention sex in the show.'

'I think you should. Most of the audience loved the whole story. They wanted the whole story. You haven't been out hurting people. I say mention it and sod their reaction.'

In the café in Leicester Square David nodded thoughtfully. 'I think we should mention it,' he said. 'I don't see the problem.'

We were in other tussles between relevance, humour and sincerity in our presentation.

Some of the girls I'd dated came to the previews. At one show, three of them turned up. Fortunately, they all enjoyed it and there was no awkwardness.

One girl I dated this year constantly told me how funny she was, that other women weren't funny and that her emails were hilarious. She didn't know, but it had been partly this boasting that turned me off her. After a preview, she came over, looking sad. 'I thought my emails were really funny,' she said, 'but the ones you read out were hilarious.' I told her I'd only read the funniest ones and that I had hundreds more that were humourless. I didn't enjoy her moment of humility.

At one preview I went for all the laughs and there was no story left. At another, I went for all the sincerity and that was too heavy. By preview six, I was beginning to get some kind of balance.

Preview seven died so badly that a necrophiliac came up to me at the bar and tried to pull me.

Preview eight went very well. Preview nine went fantastically. Preview ten received an encore.

Bring on the Festival.

Jenni: Date Four

Jenni the Boatgirl came down to join me in Southampton at the weekend. We found very little to do in Southampton and had no choice but to enjoy each other's company, which turned out to be a better option than if there had been anything to do. We wandered around town to find a good restaurant on Saturday afternoon. There were three good restaurants and they were all closed. On a busy Saturday afternoon. Madness.

We ate in an Italian restaurant which took so long serving some unpleasant food that any other plans we had were thwarted, so we spent the rest of the afternoon sleeping on each other in a park.

Jenni challenged me to slip the word 'lassitude' into my act that night. I gave her a slight nod from the stage as I said it. I nearly managed to also slip in 'pugnacious', which had become our word of the day, but was heckled just as it was about to come out.

On Sunday, we took the train back to London and had lunch in Victoria Embankment Gardens. We had fish and chips which were so dried-out and tasteless that if this had been the first ever fish and chip meal the dish would never have caught on. We hadn't had a good weekend for eating but we'd had a good weekend together.

Jenni was relaxing company and I'd certainly become very fond of her. For now, she was still dating other people and so was I. I wasn't sure if she was up for marriage and by now I should have asked her. But I hadn't even asked myself why I hadn't asked her. I enjoyed hanging out with her so much that I didn't really think of her as part of my mission.

I did think her tolerance of the unusual nature of my show might wear thin. I hoped not, but that was an entirely selfish hope. Every woman who got involved with my project knew what she was getting involved with, but it's too unusual a situation to predict how it would affect someone, including me. Jenni and I were not, at this stage, ready to move in somewhere together or to declare the relationship official, so to stop my wife-hunt at this point would have been premature. But not to stop might be stopping relationships that would need to blossom in their own time from even forming their petals naturally.

It was obvious that such dilemmas would arise with the ambitious undertaking I had embarked on. Yet it hadn't been that obvious when it started. Back in February, I received abundant warning of things that could go wrong. 'What if you meet your ideal partner on the third date? You won't have a story?' To which I would reply, 'That would be great. I'll have met my ideal partner. And it will be a short story.' I had answers for everything back then. But no one predicted the more subtle development problems. I was doing something outrageous and I expected the outcome to be equally outrageous. It would be laughs all the way; girls would find it hilarious and I'd laugh with one of them all the way to the registry office.

I wanted to spend the rest of the day with Jenni, but I had a show to write. Everyone I knew who was taking a show up to the Edinburgh fringe was working full out. They weren't going out on lots of dates and writing funny or mundane or reassuring emails to

lots of women. I'd spent all my money on this show. I'd invested all my time on this show. So I left Jenni and I went home to work. Emily had been right: whether I liked it or not, and whether anyone else liked it or not, I was married to my career.

The Murder Date

Morag had been to our house at the beginning of July with a friend of ours, and I'd met her after venturing away from my computer for a few minutes in my dressing gown. She admired my clothing choice in a way that didn't make me think she meant it. She told me we'd met before very briefly at a party. The memory eluded me, but I couldn't imagine not remembering her.

She was simply gorgeous and had such a deliciously dark sense of humour that I thought I could easily get obese on it. We laughed inwardly and talked seriously outwardly about all the people she thought should be disembowelled, which was most people, how she thought she would like to go about it, murder, the time she stole a broom (many years ago – she's grown out of such behaviour), and just how common the Wombles were. She'd heard about my mission and suggested a date. I'm not sure that I'd normally have had the nerve to ask her out, and in fact I didn't normally ask girls out, anyway. It was one of those occasions when I really loved my mission. I took her number and her email address and told her I'd contact her to arrange the date.

I sent her an email and reminded her in the heading that I was the man in the dressing gown.

Morag

I did not get a chance to call you today and because I did not want the full 24hr period to escape without me making the effort I decided to take advantage of your email. Basically, I was so enchanted by your descriptive plans to disembowel so many people (nearly everyone, I think), that the opportunity to take you out on a date seemed irresistible. If you are still up for that date, then I will phone you this week and make an arrangement. If you have changed your mind, I will still phone but to call you lily-livered.

I have to go now because a grizzly bear with attitude problems has entered my room and is trying to drag me out into the garden by my foot to meet his family and I am hardly even dressed for the occasion. It is probably my fault for sitting at my computer wearing this bear suit and for putting on that randy-female-bear perfume, which I bought today. I should have known it was cheap for a reason. Covering myself with honey was also a mistake. And putting that sign in the front garden that reads 'Hot and lonely female bear seeking company'. Still, we learn by our mistakes.

I hope I have succeeded in creating a warm and friendly atmosphere with this letter, so you better reply immediately or you're in deep shit, woman.

And I told her, 'Because I am eventually trying to find a wife out of all this dating, it is imperative that I know a few things about you. So, here is a questionnaire.'

She replied to my questionnaire with the following answers.

Q: Did you ever use the broom you stole?
A: Actually I did. Went for a quick stroll. Showed off to my friends and

popped back in the back entrance of the shop and placed it in the haberdashery department next to the trims.

Q: Would it be too late to return it and apologise?

A: I'm afraid I didn't apologise at the time. And I think an apology now could be confusing for any shop manager or cashier.

Q: Do you like gardening?

A: Yes. Very much so. Earth, seeds, water, toil, magic.

Q: Name everywhere you've been ever.

A: I've only ever been to that party the other night and a weekend break in Scunthorpe. The rest of the time I never leave my house. Why do you think I accepted this date?

Q: What time is it?

A: The time is 11.54 a.m.

Q: If I were to buy you a pet, which I am not, what would it be?

A: A dog. Always a dog. But a giraffe would also be absolutely fine, of course.

Q: How many people have you met?

A: Twelve. Mum. Dad. Brother. Sister. People at that party the other night. You. I feel complete . . . really.

Q: Why?

A: Because you must. Always.

Q: Are you thinking of the colour red?

A: Green is usually my internal thought colour.

Q: If Big Ben was not a clock but was a can of beer, what beer would it be? (Clue – Stella)

A: Um. Stella?

Q: Which of the following adjectives would you use to describe yourself (please choose at least one or none as you wish): happy, tall, short, angry, mad, sane, conspicuous, fraught, obstinate, flame-proof, Australian, inventive, confused, drunk, misanthropic, tubular, oleaginous.

A: Happy. Tubular. Conspicuous.

Q: How far can you swim under water?

A: 400 metres. I have lock-off/lock-on gills.

Q: Do you celebrate Christmas?

A: Tricky one. I give presents, eat a meal, get merry. But I don't celebrate The Birth of Baby Jesus.

Q: Where is Birmingham?

A: Next to Scunthorpe. I'm sure I passed it on the way.

She told me she hadn't replied straight away because she was shopping for hot and lonely bear costumes.

I really liked what I'd seen of Morag so far and one of the qualities I wanted to find in my wife was an unshockable sense of humour.

I am not sure what mood I was in when I sent this long reply late that evening:

Morag, your answers scored 95 per cent. You lost 5 percent with the assertion that green is your internal thought colour. It is actually a greeny-red, which you will realise to be true if you examine it a bit more carefully. Unfortunately, this means that you have not scored high enough to be my bride at this time, but you are still eligible for a date. If on the date, we fall in love at first sight, which is unlikely because we've seen each other before and I don't think you did fall in love with me, and I suspect you were only taken by my dressing gown, and I only vaguely remember having met you at some party (though I think I might have fallen in love with you when we were chatting the other day but it's hard to tell 'cos I haven't had time to think about such things because I've been too busy writing your name all over my bedroom wall, getting tattoos of you all over my body and shaping my pillow to look like you, which might disturb you a little especially if you saw the way I shaped my other pillow to look

like another girl and made the two pillows interact in a way that
could get me committed or exposed by the gutter-press, which is
most of the press, if I were famous and if I had been photographed
in action with the two pillows [though if they'd kept filming, they
would have seen that I slept well that night and instead of
denigrating me they could recommend this pillow-activity to
insomniacs and actually help people for a change]) then (just
remind you where we're up to 'cos I think the long bit in brackets
might have confused the clarity of this paragraph. It went: If on the
date, we fall in love at first sight – then there was another bit
followed by the stuff in brackets followed by then) you may take the
test again at a time of your choosing, but would be well advised to
answer greeny-red to question 9. I would also suggest that we both
smash our heads pretty hard with bricks before this date to cause a
mutual amnesia and thus give ourselves as much chance as possible
of falling in love at first sight or at least being able to lie to people
and ourselves about this as honestly as possible. Furthermore, we
should both poke one of our eyes out before the date in case we
meet another couple who claim to have fallen in love at first sight
because then we will one-up them by saying that we fell in love at
half a first sight. I hope you do not feel that I am putting too much
expectation on what is, after all, just a date, just a drink, or a meal
and a drink, or two drinks, or two meals, or whatever combination it
turns out to be – I'm simply trying to prepare myself in case it
turns out to be explosive. After all, life is unpredictable. We might
fall in love at first sight and fall in contempt at second sight. I
wonder if there have ever been two psychics who fell in love at
second-sight? So, in short, I am officially inviting you out on a date.
You may take your time thinking about it but do remember that you
have already agreed it to it anyway. If you have any hesitation on
this matter I am prepared to come round and ask you in person
wearing the Dressing Gown of Irresistibility. If I have not got you

right and you are actually like the majority of women and people of other sexes then you will have found this letter too forward, disgusting and depraved. If I have got you right and you did not find it to be those things then you should know that you are wrong because it is all those things.

One more thing, where was the shop that you stole the broom from because I think it would be good on our date to go back there together and make that apology? We could take the manager a box of chocolates and film you getting this whole filthy episode out of your system so that you can carry on with your life. I think it would be a touching moment in my show that would help the audience see that even if my project does not find me a wife at least it has helped people along the way.

One more one more thing, I could not call you today even though I desperately wanted to (pause – this letter is beginning to look suggestively like I am actually infatuated with you and not just being tongue-in-cheek. Please relax, I am not infatuated with you although I have to admit that the tongue-in-cheek that I'm imagining I'm being is actually an imagined image of my tongue in your cheek [and that comment was tongue-in-cheek too {and I apologise for getting into bracket-complications}]. I was saying that I desperately wanted to call you today but couldn't because:) I had to keep my phone line open for some urgent stuff to do with this show. Tomorrow is an insane day but I will try to call you before you have a chance to read this letter in case it makes you change all your contact details.

Stay happy, tubular and conspicuous, which is how I like you, until we next meet and please remember that anything you write to me can and will be used against you in my book. If you are innocent, you have nothing to fear.

OK, I think I have bared my soul enough, which does not bother me because I stole this soul, so hope to speak soon and that it is to you when it happens and please just try and get on with your life as best as you can whilst you are awaiting my call. Maybe get a friend to sit by the phone with you.

I didn't call her the next day because there wasn't a good time to talk and because there were so many plans moving around that I was waiting to find a window to arrange the date for.

She replied. I stared at my inbox for some moments, not wanting to open her email because I thought she might say my email was too lots of things. Here is her reply:

Many thanks for your recent epistle with its creative, energetic use of brackets and the frankly incredible pillow-talk. I am also pleased that I passed your questions with an element of success. A dating we shall go, ho ho. I also see now that I might have some red thought matter round the edges of the green – thank you for this insight. It's a beautiful thing.

In regards to the tattoos, have you just been scripting my name with accompanying roses, thorns, hearts etc? You see, I'm hoping that you are going to say you now have an enormous picture of my face on your chest with nipples for eyes. I'd appreciate it if you could clear this up for me.

In the matter of the request for me to present box of chocolates to a bewildered shop manager with a purge-worthy, self-flagellating style apology for broom theft (actually more of a broom-borrow) – this has all the hallmarks of a Morag Humiliation Moment, and could even lead to me being disowned by family and friends, cast out to sip the bitter cup of Rejection and Despair. Basically, I'll think about it, Marx.

Also, in advance of the date, I was wondering if you had any advice on removing an eyeball? I'm particularly interested in creating the most sensational noise as it pops out so I would imagine something with suction would be most effective … The only other option would be to see if a passing crow would be so kind as to peck it out for me. I presume your idea for the mutual eyeball removal is so that we can literally exchange eyes at the potential future marriage ceremony? Frankly Carey, that's so damn beautiful I'm nearly welling up.

I feel I should warn you that a date with Morag usually features some kind of act of mindless violence. Basically it's always worth bringing with you a pair of wellies, some duct tape, and any local information you may have on the abandoned quarries, wasteland or woods around the area. For my part, I'll bring my usual roll of bin bags and portable flame-thrower.

Boy are we gonna have some fun.

Another thing. All potential Morag-dates need to let me know their weapon of choice –

Bayonet

Rolling boulder

Wok

Other [requires explanation]

As I have no alive friends, it may only be possible to sit with my imaginary one at the time of your telephone call to organise our 'date experience'. In which case, I will have my smelling salts to hand in case of one of my 'turns'. I look forward to your call and hope you are in a pleasant, uplifted, mildly joyous mood.

I replied,

Morag,

My letter to you was clearly just fun, but I find your response to be depraved and, frankly, shocking. I have shown your letter to the police and the social services and they are all coming after you.

OK, that's not true, but it bothers me that you see through me so easily. Nothing makes me happier than a good wok-murder date with a rolling-boulder-person-splattering coming in a close second. And, yes, I do know how to make an eye ball pop on exit. It's all in the thumb movement.

I did not call you this weekend for various reasons one of which is that I was not in the requested pleasant, uplifted, mildly joyous mood. I will be tomorrow for sure. I can assure you, however, that I am about to write in the book, which is an as honest as I can make it account of relevant events in my search for my ideal woman, that arranging this date with you is a top priority.

Hope to speak to you in a few hours. Don't kill anyone without me.

Arranging a date with Morag was a top priority because here was definitely my type of girl. So I wanted to come up with a murder date that would impress her. In the back of my mind I wanted to be vindicated for the Cyclops fiasco by organising the date properly and leaving no room for misunderstanding.

In the evening, I wrote some emails to various people who might help me organise a murder. One of several plans was this: while Morag and I are having lunch she receives a phone call from someone saying, 'I need help – someone's trying to kill me.' We have to collect a suitcase from a locker and follow clues that take us across France, over to Switzerland, then to Amsterdam and finally back to London. During all this we get arrested and the police bring out the emails Morag sent me as damning evidence. We are released and continue on our mission. Our mission is not actually to save the man's life. Instead we are conspiring to make sure he gets killed. In the end, we discover his dead and bloody body and we celebrate.

This all turned out to be far more complicated to arrange than I was expecting and friends of mine in the various countries were not going to be around on the day to help out.

I had another plan, which was to let Morag kill someone. This plan required specialist special-effects equipment including an exploding body-blood-bag. But, a special-effects company I used to know had shut down and I couldn't find another with the equipment.

Every idea I had for our murder date led me nowhere, because each was too ambitious. Then, at a gig the night before the date, a man called Greg made a suggestion: why didn't we play the winking game in Trafalgar Square? Morag and I would walk around winking at people and they would fall over and die. The winking game did not feel like enough for me, but the idea developed into one where we shot a gun in a park. Everyone in the park, including a tramp on a bench and some lovers by a tree, would fall over and die. In the present climate in London this would have been far too risky. A policeman might run over and shoot us in the head and that had never been a romantic thing to happen on a date. I needed to find a room for it to happen in.

Back home, I told the idea to Phil. He suggested a test tube of a mysterious substance instead of the gun. Now the plan had become almost feasible.

In the morning, I emptied a box of some of my old magic props onto the floor, found a test tube and filled it with ash. On the way to the date, I rang my secretary, Janice. I told her I needed her to find a room somewhere in central London that we could use at 8 p.m. I also needed people and I needed them to be ready to choke to death on cue. She said that she would make it happen. I popped into a chemist and bought some surgical facemasks.

I met Morag at 1 p.m. in a pub that had made a lot of money out of my dating. We chatted over several drinks and I apologised for failing to organise a murder date. I told her of some of my attempts. Then I told her about a friend of mine who has many shady friends, one of whom had become very interested in my murder date and had taken it very seriously. I couldn't tell whether he was being serious in a tongue-in-cheek way or if he really was so serious. He offered to help me get hold of something. He was very strange; he wouldn't even tell me his name. Just before I came out on this date, I explained, a motorcycle courier had arrived at my home and dropped off this test tube and these two masks, which he said had been treated with a chemical for protection.

Morag asked what was in the test tube. I called it Benefalio215, though bene is a prefix meaning good. You must understand that I sold this tale with a naïve-seeming confusion that employed many methods I've learnt to use as a magician. I even let her handle the test tube. She agreed that we shouldn't open it. I told her I'd rung one of my connections who works as a forensics investigator for the police. 'I am sure it's nothing, really,' I told her, 'but I should get it checked out just in case that guy is a real nutter.'

We got on great. Morag may have a darker sense of humour than most people who think they have a dark sense of humour, but her humour is far too rounded to be filed with that label alone and she has the ability to instantly become earnest as required. We laughed a lot. We talked about the recent death of her mother and the less recent death of my father, and that conversation was quite fascinating and revealing with its even points of view and lack of drama. I enjoyed the way our conversation flowed easily between funny and serious points. She told me that a few days ago she'd been in a hotel room getting drunk with a friend and they'd rung down to reception and ordered some puppies. A short time later, they rang again and ordered some clowns. Some time later, they rang again and ordered some children.

We decided to have a murder-theme day, seeing as I hadn't organised a murder, and chose such events as Madame Tussauds, the London Dungeon and a play with a murder in it. Morag wanted to see if we could find some trolls and suggested that we have a look under bridges.

We went off to find food and ended up having quite a long but very funny walk around Covent Garden. We tried some perfumes in an expensive-perfume shop. I asked the lady assistant whether large people or short people had to wear different perfumes because their skin is different. She took me seriously with a long speech in which she absolutely assured us several times that this was not so. We wandered into a Mediterranean restaurant that was the most ostentatiously decorated place I had ever wandered into. Morag asked if they served troll. They didn't. We wandered back out.

As we walked through Leicester Square we saw a troll. He was squat, with fat legs which he had obviously shaved as a disguise.

We had a Chinese lunch, and whenever Morag went to the toilet or I did, I exchanged text messages with Janice to see how she was doing. She'd found a room upstairs in a pub that we could have for free and had found the people. One text said, 'Everything is ready to go, you romantic fool'.

We took a cab to the London Dungeon. We bought tickets and asked if there were going to be any clowns. We were told there would not be. We asked about trolls. Again, no. We asked about actors. Yes, there would be actors. A couple of the exhibits were fun but the tour seemed to be aimed at children, although there was only one child in the group that we were forced to walk round with. In each room an actor with black eyes and a few facial scars leapt out and presented a less than scary talk which was not lacking in scariness for want of over trying. We agreed that it was only scary if you were afraid of actors.

'Actor alert!' became our catchphrase. I don't think that we were a good audience. I am sure, however, that the actors knew we'd soon get too bored to bother heckling, and this did indeed happen after about half an hour. It was a good kind of shared bored, though, and at one point I suggested we should open the test tube. Morag said we should not.

On the way out, we bought some scars and then caught a cab back into London. We went to Kettners for a drink and to put on our scars.

Janice sent me a text to tell me that the group would be ready for us at 8 p.m. (Later, I discovered that she already had everyone in the room practising the death scene.)

At 8 p.m. we entered the pub, the Bath House, that had kindly allowed us to use their upstairs room for free. As we walked into the room, I spotted housemate Matt. He lifted a newspaper over his face and fortunately was not seen by Morag, who knew him. She also knew housemate Nick, whom neither of us spotted, and housemate Eva, who was disguised in a giant blond wig and sitting with her back to us. The room was full of people chatting over drinks.

At the bar, we asked about the play. The barmaid assured us that she didn't know anything about a play. We asked if there was anything going on tonight involving trolls or clowns. There wasn't. 'Let's go and sit down,' suggested Morag. I stayed at the bar and calmly called her back, because I'd been told to stand in this spot for the hidden camera. She came back. I suggested we open the test tube.

She said no.

I said I couldn't believe that it really contained anything.

She agreed.

We put on the facemasks.

I passed her the test tube and told her to open it. She hesitated for some time.

When she did open it, nothing happened at first. Then the barmaid started coughing. Morag closed the test tube. I reopened it, pretending not to notice anything going on. A man leaning on the bar started coughing. The coughing spread around the room and then people started dying. One man spat out half a pint of beer as he collapsed; another went down in slow motion, holding his throat. A woman fell off her chair. Moments later, all thirteen people in the room were dead. Morag looked shocked. I suggested we get out of there. She agreed and stepped over the bodies on her way to the door. Then she was moving fast. I had to run after her and I caught up with her outside the room. 'I told you I'd give you a murder date,' I said.

Her face changed instantly to sheer delight but it had changed so quickly that some of the shock was still on show. She said, 'Oh, Carey, you're lovely. Oh my god. No one's done that for me before. Oh my GOD. I was terrified. I was absolutely terrified.'

She came back into the room as all the dead people stood up and she recognised and hugged those she knew. She also used some strong language. Later, she said that she'd smelt smoke when people started coughing – an interesting psychosomatic effect. My friends had certainly been much better actors than the real ones at the London Dungeon.

We all had a few drinks together and it was clear that Morag was impressed. She took the stunt with glee. Whatever you think of Morag from my description of her, I think she's brilliant.

We went back to Kettners for a pizza. She insisted on paying, which to be honest I was grateful for because my funds were in a bad state by this time. At the last count, I'd spent six thousand pounds on dating and then I'd stopped counting. We moved on for a last drink at a private club which had given me membership because I performed a preview there. We were given two bottles of wine for free. We sat with the staff after closing time. I showed them some card tricks. Morag read their fortunes with blatant bullshit patter. Though they all knew she was bullshitting, they each wanted a turn, and one of them insisted that the reading was spot on.

It had been a fantastic date. However, I knew Morag wasn't going to marry me. During our Chinese lunch she'd told me that she had recently started seeing someone, another comedian. I think she thought that I knew about this, because some of my housemates had been at the party where they met (since I'd asked her out). I think I'd missed this piece of information because I'd been too wrapped up in my own world to be aware of the goings on among friends. Morag explained that she'd still wanted to come out on this murder date, and that the man she was seeing thought it funny and didn't mind. I couldn't complain, especially as I was seeing lots of women. Also, I was enjoying her company so much that end results were irrelevant and as far as I was concerned it had just become a mate date.

Before we parted company, Morag told me that my organising a murder had been the most romantic thing anyone had done for her. And she said we'd be friends for a long time. In that, I think she is right.

Lesson

I am romantic. Before this year, I never would have thought that to be true. Morag's suggestion that I'd done something romantic made me think. And what I thought was: I am truly romantic. What I have done this year is romantic.

Very suddenly, I stopped seeing my mission as the methodologically conducted experiment that I'd wanted it to be, or the cheap game show challenge that others wanted it to be, and I saw it for what it truly was. A man's realisation

that he is romantic and that, as a result of a daft idea and
some outside pushing, he was on a journey of self-discovery.
He was on a journey from a stale single existence that
festered with denial to a wonderful place full of promise and
thrill. In that moment of realisation, I felt very happy to be
that man.

I'd intended to test every form of dating so that I could give a
thorough view of the dating scene. So far, I had attempted to go
speed-dating but the events were always on evenings when I was
working or had dates arranged. I also wanted to see what results a
small ad in a paper would receive. Janice put one in *Time Out* for me.

The ad said very little but it did receive around twelve responses
within a week of coming out. I never managed to meet any of the
respondents. I had way too many emails to deal with already.

Towards the end of July, I finally admitted that writing individual
replies to all the new women contacting me was impossible. I sent out
a group email apologising, and said that if any of them were in
London on the coming Sunday, the day before I was to travel to
Edinburgh, I'd hang around in a pub all afternoon and buy them all
drinks. I promised I'd do my best to see that it was fun and didn't feel
like a group interview, and would arrange staggered times so that I
could see them individually for at least half an hour each. I knew it
would leave me just as staggered before my last preview in Kingston,
but I couldn't, having come this far, lose a last opportunity to see if
the girl of my dreams would show up just before the Festival.

I received a large number of replies, wrote back to these ladies
individually and arranged seven dates. Those seven dates would take
the number of dates I had since the start of the mission including all

the mini-dates in and around gigs, to a hundred. A good number to go up to the Festival with.

On the day of the seven dates, however, I found myself on a train which developed a mechanical fault. We heard constant announcements of delays and were shafted out onto a station at Didcot Parkway.

As the delay grew longer, I realised that the plan was off and I rang each of my dates to cancel. They were all very nice about it, and three of them sounded so good on the phone that I regretted not having a chance to meet them, especially because I wouldn't have another chance before leaving for the Festival.

The Book

I'd tried to write the book during odd moments on the way to gigs or between keeping up with the never-ending emailing. Every computer glitch, bug, virus and mystery that could happen happened. By the end of July the story I'd written was a gibbering mush of loose thoughts.

'How's the book going?' asked David.

'Horrible. I either have to find time to write it more clearly or change the title to *And Then I.*'

'How long do you have?' he asked.

'My deadline's the beginning of September. I have to write the rest and try and make what I've written as coherent as possible before then.'

'When can you do that?'

'I'll have to find time up at the Festival.'

The Show

I bought a screen and projector just before leaving for Edinburgh and had no idea how to use them. I had the movie of the murder-date with

Morag, which was hilarious. Plus, I intended to film my crucial decision-making dates with Holly, Jenni, and Mia in Edinburgh and play them in the show. I planned to have film showing as the audience came in and some other relevant pieces of film during the show, such as an amusing skit in which I was exercising and preparing to be eligible.

'When are we going to make those films?' asked David.

'We'll have to find time up at the Festival.'

The Commitments

I'd claimed that I'd learn a romantic poem, learn to cook an exciting dish, stop smoking, get fit, dress better and take fighting lessons to protect my wife. At some point I'd let all this go because I hadn't expected to become so busy. These commitments had become gimmicks on the mission's back, which could easily have broken its spine. By the end of July, I'd even started smoking again.

'I'm still going to try and achieve them all,' I told David.

'When are you going to do all that?' he asked.

'I guess I'll have to find time up at the Festival.'

End-of-July Report

I'd had ninety-three dates and spent a few months meeting beautiful, intelligent and funny women. There had been a few duds along the way, but relatively few.

My understanding of and comfort with romance were now well-formed talents that I easily displayed. I hadn't become a fan of romantic novels or soggy films but had found romance to be something far broader than its popular manifestations.

Here's a bad example of romance, which one of the girls I dated told me. She'd been bent over the bed while her boyfriend was having sex with her from behind. She said, 'Do you love me?' and he replied, 'I'm fuckin' you, ain't I?'

OK, not great romance but to be honest I'd have to shake his hand for a great answer.

I was going up to Edinburgh with confidence. My mission could not fail. There were three girls I'd be happy to marry. Plus, all the press attention guaranteed an abundance of possible wives at the Festival. Girls who'd know exactly what I was about and would enjoy being involved in my endeavour. Success was in my sights.

THE EDINBURGH FESTIVAL
AND MADNESS

As I stepped onto the train for Edinburgh I prepared my mind for the grand finale of my mission. I would find a wife during the Festival. The success of the show was paramount to my mission: my pride was embedded in it. I wanted all the women I'd dated to realise they'd taken part in a great thing. A stupendously great thing.

On the four-and-a-half-hour journey I would read some notes Janice had made for me about marriage, write some of the book, and prepare the show. I took my seat, opened a new laptop computer I'd bought the day before especially, and fell asleep for the rest of the journey.

I arrived at the venue I would be performing in and my heart sank until it bifurcated at the top of my legs and landed in each of my feet. The room had been changed since I'd last seen it. The bar had been removed, the stage had been moved, and the seating had been arranged in two long rectangular atmosphere-killing boxes which stretched out to the sides of the stage. There were some seats in front of the stage, but they didn't make the room any more friendly.

There'd be nowhere to put a projector screen that the audience would be able to see. Much of my intended presentation would be ruined and I couldn't find a way round any of the problems because there wasn't one.

For four hours, I paced up and down crushing my heart under my feet. It bled all over the stage.

Speed Dating

A man from the BBC rang me and asked if I wanted to go speed dating for a TV show. That seemed like a good idea. It would get more publicity for my show and give me a chance to test speed dating.

'We're going with a premise based on what [he named someone. Perhaps it was someone famous? I hadn't read a paper or anything all year] said about men being funnier than women. The idea is that you go round dating with Lizzie—'

I stopped him. I know Lizzie. She's hilarious. And I didn't want to prove that men are funnier than women because in my show I wanted to talk about some of the very funny women I'd met.

'OK,' he said, 'new premise. How about you go round the tables doing your act and we show how comedy woos women?'

I told him that I'd become quite experienced at dating and that women aren't impressed by a comedian performing his act to them during a date. The term 'good listener' is often heard when describing a good date, and no one loves a show-off.

'Right, how about you just go round dating the women and we film it?'

'Sounds good. They do know you're going to be filming them, don't they?'

'Yes. We've sent out a memo to the speed daters and we'll make a speech reassuring them before we start.'

His last sentence reminded me of my innocence a few months earlier. 'They won't want to be filmed,' I told him authoritatively. 'Women find dating embarrassing.'

'Trust me,' he said. 'We know what we're doing.'

'OK,' I said, recalling the time I'd thought it would be that easy.

A car took Lizzie and me to Glasgow, and we were led into a bar where the event would take place.

Before the session began, the producer made a very nice announcement, assuring the speed daters that if they let themselves be filmed he wouldn't use the footage to denigrate them in any way. I listened to his very nice speech and shook my head in a knowing way because I knew.

I travelled around the room, spending my four minutes with different women and being amused at how they turned away from the camera. The cameraman tried all kinds of reassurances, but to no avail. Two women ran off and hid in the loos as I approached their tables with the cameraman.

He persuaded a few women to let him film me over their shoulders, and promised that nothing more than a tuft of their hair would be visible. They still clammed up and made me do all the talking – it looked as if I was chatting myself up. None of them liked me, because I was embarrassing them. When I reached Lizzie's table we openly talked for the camera. We were disgusting.

I did enjoy the event, but it was extremely unnatural with a camera next to me. I ticked three girls. Then I met one whom I triple-ticked and who also made me untick the previously ticked ones. Her name was Nicole. She stopped me on the way out, to check that I'd ticked her. I would have liked to hang around and talk to her, but I was whisked off back to Edinburgh for a rehearsal of my show. Again the performing got in the way of my hunt for romance. I had created a monster. The monster that was my mission had one redeeming factor: it had a pretty face. But it kept wanting me to scratch its hairy back.

Speed dating with a BBC cameraman was a paradigm of my whole endeavour to find a wife while writing a book and a show about it. I can recommend speed dating for other people but my experience was frustrated and unnatural. The producer was a nice man and I am sure he'll cut the film to look good, but it won't paint an accurate picture of speed dating because it won't reveal the embarrassment that daters feel. It would be hard to make a film about that factor unless it was a movie showing empty seats.

Many of the men allowed themselves to be filmed talking to Lizzie, and I wondered whether the embarrassment factor was chiefly a female thing. Sisters, I demand equal rights for you. Stand up and be proud of yourselves for having a date. Men have no more right to that pride than you. Being single and looking for a partner is not a crime.

The Previews

The first two nights of the Edinburgh Festival are half-price preview shows. I asked that no reporters be allowed in for them, which is quite normal. However, signals got crossed and I was informed that I had six important publications coming in for these two nights. With all our technical problems, I was in a panic.

A reporter called late in the afternoon. He asked lots of questions and I didn't know if I was tired but it felt as though I was on the back foot. I couldn't tell for sure if he was being interested or critical, but it felt sorely critical. He said he'd like to interview some of my potential wives. I said I'd promised I wouldn't put any of them in that position. He said something about the types of women who contact prisoners. I couldn't see the connection. It was hardly the same as a woman who was amused by the idea of having a date with a comedian with intention to marriage.

The call finished, leaving me barely enough time to feed on a nasty take-away burger before running over to the venue for my show. The fifteen-minute room change-over between the preceding show and mine was filled with technical problems. I went on stage confused, and stumbled with the show in places. It was as much fun as parachuting into a field of cacti.

Preview two was plagued with new problems. It was not a good night for the press to be in. After the first ten minutes, the front row stood up and left. I thought they hated my performance, but it transpired that the front of house staff had let them into the wrong show. It did not look good. Nothing looked good.

I had a bad feeling. If this show went down, my whole mission would go down with it. I'd spent half a year prising women away from their fear of embarrassment by assuring them they wouldn't be badly represented in my show. If the show itself became an embarrassment, how many of them would still be happy to say they were involved in it?

Showtime

'We've got a lot of problems,' I told David, 'and they seem insurmountable.'

'The trouble is,' he said, 'everyone's expecting wildly different things from you. Some want romance. Some just want to laugh. Some want serious. Some want a story. Some people want to see a competition. People are coming in with too many preconceptions of what they think it's supposed to be.'

'We only have an hour. We need to change something.'

His face blanked as if he didn't want to waste on expressions an energy which could more efficiently be used thinking. Then he lit up. 'Let's let them ask questions,' he said.

I stormed into the venue with attitude. I tossed the microphone and its stand off the stage, and decided to work without them. I dumped the projection screen at the side of the stage and decided that it would just be used for a three-minute piece of film at the end. I breathed in my new-found working space. I had a lovely show, which I should have known would happen because of the absence of reviewers. I performed the whole show as a question-and-answer session to an up-beat audience who had good questions. The feedback from the audience after the show was very gratifying.

Sunday's show was another superb one. Everything was coming together. Now, if I could only find a bride ... Holly had left a message to say she would be coming up. So had Jenni the Boatgirl. Mia was also planning a visit for the end of the Festival. She regularly sent me very silly text messages concerning whatever she was up to. Here is one: 'Sign in the park: Please Do Not Feed The Ducks as it Encourages the Rats. I want to know what it encourages them to do and why I should be discouraging. What if I fed the ducks rat poison?'

I answered: 'It encourages the rats to feed the ducks and they're really nasty. They only feed the fat ones and leave the little ones to starve.'

Then there was this one: 'If it is at all possible, avoid getting to know the people behind the puppets at a children's show.' And this one: 'If you had to choose would you prefer silly, sexy or sympathetic?' to which I replied that I'd choose silly every time because you always know where you stand with silly. She responded, 'Agreed but I meant if you had to choose from a selection of muffins.'

Press Coverage

The coverage continued to smother me and I had a full diary of interviews and photo sessions. I kept thinking I should turn them all away and concentrate on the book, the show and the mission. And then I kept thinking that I had to publicise the show first and find time for all those other things when I could. Perhaps a touch of insanity was starting to flower, because it soon reached the stage where every time someone rang me with a new commitment I would grimace and giggle.

I had an interview and photo session for the *Scotsman* newspaper with another act called Matt, who was also doing a show about dating. His show concerned the methods for gaining a date suggested by self-help books. He would be in the same venue as me and was experiencing the same problems with the showing of video. We were taken outside for our photo session, which involved the two of us surrounded by some very attractive girls who were told to fawn all over us, and did. It was a good photo session but could have lasted longer, I think.

The *Daily Record* took me out on the street for an interview and some dates they set up with women they found. The dates and the interview turned out to be fun but I then had a somewhat cheesy photo with each of these women in which I had to be on bended knee pretending to propose. The interviewer asked each of them how I'd been as a date. Apparently they were all complimentary.

I particularly liked a couple of them, but one vanished as I was having another date, and I didn't ask for the other one's number because I didn't want her to associate me with the cheese that had brought us together. Besides, no matter how lovely these girls were, I didn't think it fair to Mia, Jenni and Holly to consider more dates. I had to be strong. Next I had a photo-session for *The Times*. The photograph involved more attractive women and more fawning. I put up with it gallantly.

Forces Radio interviewed me one afternoon. I'd planned to talk about the show in a way that the forces would relate to, by using expressions like 'my mission', 'the dating battleground', 'taking no prisoners', 'firing a cannonball of effort through the wall of empty one-night stands', 'tiptoeing through the minefield of nutters' and using 'intelligence to see through the camouflage of the base where my love is held captive', but I think the interviewer knew I was up to mischief so he fired a few fast questions at me and said goodbye.

The press write-ups I received all reinforced the original notion of my mission. I was trying to find a wife by the end of the Festival. Some of them ridiculed me for being so ambitious. This spurred me forward even more furiously. I would definitely do it. There was still more than three weeks to go. Easy.

Dates

If I include the dates set up by newspapers, I'd reached a hundred and twenty dates on my mission. I'd been in written communication with over two hundred women. I continued going through the motions of dating, mainly to satisfy my Edinburgh audience but I knew I wouldn't marry someone I met at such short notice.

Getting drunk with girls was too costly. An audience wouldn't accept me performing drunk, unrehearsed or hungover because I had been on dates.

Dating was pointless. For a long time my story had felt like a story about a story getting in the way of the story. I had no choice but call a moratorium on the dating.

Reviews, Wave One

The Edinburgh reviewers are a constant complaint of the acts. We who are new or newish to the Festival need good reviews to attract audiences away from the myriad other choices of shows and bigger names. There are some proficient reviewers, who see entertainment all year round, but most are given the job just for the Festival and have little clue about it.

A spate of bad reviews based on the preview nights hit me hard.

They claimed the show had bad direction because the audience had to move to watch the video. I should be showing more video of the dates and of ones at the Festival. These criticisms were of elements out of my control.

Newspaper articles had also changed their tune. They came down on me heavily for having a gimmick theme for a show. But the gimmick part of it was the very reason they were all talking about me.

It was going to be a gruelling job to bring the show out of its floundering start to the Festival while we had to wait for all those other reviews born of the two nightmare previews to clobber us harder. Along with this, among the nice comments in various articles there was also a certain amount of cynicism. Who would have thought that my nice little mission would get such a mixed reception?

Holly

Holly was in town. Boisterously excited about seeing her, I ran off half way through an interview. I was going to marry the shit out of her.

I would propose to her on stage that night. A travel company had offered two tickets to Vegas for an instant wedding. David had boxes of confetti backstage for the audience to throw.

We had a few drinks in the theatre bar. I had trouble making her laugh. I asked what was wrong.

She told me she cared a lot about me.

I asked again what was wrong.

She asked why I didn't mind all the press I was getting and suggested I was thriving on it.

'To some extent, that's true,' I said. 'We come here to get noticed, and I've been noticed. I know some of them think what I'm doing is cheap, but it's still publicity.'

'Is that how you really feel?'

It took me a while to understand that she wasn't simply talking about how the publicity affected me. 'I know how some people are viewing my show,' I told her, 'and to some extent they are right. I couldn't completely remove the gimmick from an idea like this, though I tried to de-gimmick it as much as I could. I became fascinated by the real experiment and wanted to see if it would work. If I hadn't spent my year doing this, we'd never have met.'

'I know.'

'Come and see the show. It'll give you a clearer perspective than the reviews.'

'I'm not staying. I just came up here to tell you why I don't want to do this any more.'

She told me that she couldn't understand why I was so indifferent to everything that was being said. I told her that both good and bad was being said.

The biggest public fear is public speaking. That's one reason why so many people are embarrassed about dating or asking for a date. Everyone is afraid of what other people might think. Comedians think they are above that and yet, even if we have had an obviously amazing gig and received an encore, we still relish the audience members who come up afterward and say, 'That was great.' If we didn't need that, we wouldn't do the job. But we also have to take the bad days. The last time I'd met Holly she'd said she couldn't understand how we stay on stage when people shout insults. My mission had become bigger than I'd expected, and she no longer felt comfortable with the possibility of being thrown into the limelight.

'Holly, this is still tiny,' I told her. 'Nothing much has changed. I've been honest with you from the start.'

'I know that. But you don't get it. What you're doing has become a circus. You can't win. Even if you do marry someone, no one will believe it's genuine. They'll say your wife is a gimmick and think you're even cheaper. And she'll have to answer lots of questions.'

'No. Honestly. You're overestimating the interest in me. I'm doing this for me now. If I get married there'll be a few sceptics, but so what? I don't care what people think.'

Something very unfortunate happened at that moment. A man in the bar came over and, quite playfully, asked if I was going to be marrying Holly. He kept it going too long. I laughed him away.

Holly told me that she wanted to see me if I did not marry anyone. But only a long time after all this was over.

As I watched her leave, I knew that my relationship with her was over. At first, I tore at myself for not saying the right things to calm her fears. Later, I saw it differently. She was worried about being judged. But in my business being judged is unavoidable. I need a wife who will stick with me when things are rough. She is a great girl. She is fantastic. But she wasn't my wife, and it was better that I'd found that out.

'I'm not enjoying it,' I told David. 'The press are now laying into me for thinking I could get married by the end of the Festival. Holly's walked out. It's all become unpleasant. I'm going to leave for a few days. Not because I can't handle it all, but because I don't see why I should have to take all this bullshit. I haven't seen my nephews and nieces all year. I'm going to go to Spain and see them. I'll cancel the show for a few days.'

'It's not a bad idea, actually. It might add to all the publicity. I expect a lot of rumours will go round.'

I realised I couldn't leave: it would be seen as another publicity stunt. Anything I did now would be seen as a publicity stunt. If I got married, it would be seen as a publicity stunt. I knew what Holly had meant.

In the evening I had another great show with a full audience but it didn't make me happy. There were five minutes of chaos as I moved a third of the audience to another part of the room to watch the video.

Then gradually came the very complimentary reviews. One said I was witty, sincere, interesting, and unique and I had the capacity to keep you on the edge of your seat while laughing so hard you might fall off it. It asked if I was a genius or a lunatic.

Jenni the Boatgirl arrived in Edinburgh the next day. On the way to meeting her at the station, I bumped into a couple called Brian Damage and Krysstol who were performing at the fringe. They said they'd been looking for me to tell me something relevant to my quest. They'd met at the fringe some years ago and got engaged five days later. They were married within a month. Anything is possible.

It was brilliant to have Jenni around. She came to the show. 'I don't get all the negativity,' she said afterward. 'It's such a fun show. It has an uplifting message. I don't see what those critics were on about.'

We drank until late.

Over the next couple of days I had large and fabulous audiences at the show, and for the third time met a group of people who had been twice. Feedback afterward was all positive. The show was for the public, not the reviewers. My mission was for me and for anyone who could take something sweet from it. Anyone getting a sour taste from my message was eating their own bad grapes.

I had a great few days with Jenni before she left. I didn't know why, but I let her go without asking her to marry me.

Reviews, Wave Two

On 16 August, I had a day off and a chance to think about a strategy to bring my mission to its great finale. I'd been in regular communication with Mia, and I had the feeling that our relationship had naturally become a strong friendship. I treasured this friendship and was happy to accept that achievement.

I had an idea on how I would end my mission.

There was still one big hope in the form of Nicole, the speed-dating girl. I'd only known her for four minutes, and perhaps I was building my hopes too high. I might be adding fantasy to reality; I might have become an emotional wreck and unable to see clearly. But there was also a chance I was right to pin my hopes on Nicole. We got on very well in those few minutes. I liked her look. I liked her voice. No, I wasn't wrong. I would definitely like her, she would like me and we would get married. So there.

Then I read a review by a guy called Chris Bartlett in *The Stage* and it made me MAD. He said my show was not about love but about a 'laddish personal task'.

My life is a personal task. When I put on a pair of shoes, that is a personal task. If I were to set myself the task of trying lots of different nuts to see which nuts I like best and people found that personal task interesting and encouraged me to report on my findings, what would be wrong with me reporting on my findings? How can anyone say such an endeavour is not about nuts? Is a personal task not about the thing that the personal task is about because being a personal task cancels out the subject matter of the personal task?

Is it laddish behaviour to try and find a wife?

'There are also', said the review, 'the moral implications of dating some 150 women and sleeping with some of them for the sole reason of accruing material for a comedy show.'

I slept with women for material? And I slept with them for that *sole* reason? Deeply upset about this accusation, I called a friend and in my anger I declared, 'I have never slept with a woman for entertainment!'

For the next couple of days I was a little stroppy. Not a lot stroppy.

I didn't go around being rude to people. In fact, I smiled and laughed a lot. My inner strop was fuelled by other comments that came out in the press. One reporter said that I had 'such cynical conceit, it's depressing'.

Still the accusations came. A reviewer wrote, 'The quest led him to arrange extravagant and imaginative dates in graveyards with existentialist nihilists and to fake mass murder in a London pub to impress another equally troubled lady.'

I didn't then understand why all this was getting to me. But I do now. Cyclops had been proven right. Holly was right. I don't know how Cyclops would react to being called 'troubled', but I expect Morag would find it funny. Cyclops wasn't what I'd taken her to be, but I didn't think she was 'troubled'. At least I had given her a pseudonym to take the abuse. Morag is Morag's real name and I didn't want Morag being called 'troubled' when I think she's wonderful. How dare he cast aspersions on her character because he saw cynicism in me? All she did was go out on an amusing date.

These reviewers had no right to throw abuse at my new friends. Handling bad press is one thing. Feeling responsible for causing it to someone else is different. That was the root of my depression.

Reviews, Wave Three

The next few days brought a spate of very nice reviews. They quoted parts of my show and got the quotes right. Now I was hearing that '*Marry Me* is, without doubt, an original and entertaining show, which keeps the audience amused throughout the act.' The stories were described as 'hilarious dating shenanigans' and my murder date was now 'ingenious'. I had 'real comic flair and enough charm to keep the audience hooked'.

I was happy with that. I thought Holly would call any moment and say that she'd been wrong. Not all the press are bad. And Eddie

Harrison, from *Metro*, truly got the show: 'Despite using dating as a subject for comedy, it's obvious that Marx is a romantic at heart . . . Even if it involves murdering a bar full of innocent people or bringing a graveyard of zombies back to life, there's absolutely nothing he won't do for a girl.'

My audience numbers increased.

Overall, the show had received roughly equal amounts of glowing and cutting reviews, and I began to realise that for better or worse I'd achieved a fair amount of notoriety. As I walked along a street people would ask me if I were married yet. Some were genuinely interested and hopeful; others were making fun of me. People told me they'd enjoyed my show and had recommended it to their friends. People told me my show was awful and I was exploiting women. One woman came right across the room in a bar to tell me that no one would ever want to marry me; she hadn't even seen the show. Several people told me I had changed their view of dating for the better. A man told me I was sick. Another man told me that he'd asked a girl out as a result of seeing my show. From one end of a street to another, my mood could change as much as ten times.

I bumped into a man who said he'd seen the show and accused me of making fun of the institution of marriage. I asked him to tell me which bit had upset him, and he couldn't. For some people, a comedian broaching a subject must mean that the comedian is belittling that subject.

Many people had dramatic opinions and I could never make sense of the extreme reactions I'd caused. Three women I'd dated rang me after seeing the Bartlett review. Two were offended by how his suggestion that I'd been exploiting women reflected on them. They assured me he was talking nonsense. The third thought it was hilarious. 'What's wrong with exploiting women, anyway?' she wanted to know. 'It's the best thing to do with them.'

Mia arrived. She was unconcerned about Bartlett and in her characteristically measured manner told me that I shouldn't be, either. She joined a comedy course to see what it was all about and told me that a man on her course said he'd seen my show and it had changed his attitude to romance. He now realised that romance was for everyone.

One evening, I walked out of a bar in one of the venues and a girl came over and told me she'd seen my show. 'I was disgusted,' she said. 'It was horrible how you're exploiting women.'

'Explain that to me,' I implored her. 'I keep hearing that from people but I don't understand. How am I exploiting women?'

'I don't know,' she replied, 'but you are.'

At that moment Morag, who was at the Festival to see her boyfriend, James, was passing. She gently held the girl's arms and said, 'If women are the pathetic, fragile creatures you think we are, I don't want to be one. Carey and I are friends. We became friends in minutes and we had a great day out.'

The girl had tears on her face. 'Thank you . . . thank you . . . ' she said to Morag.

'What am I dealing with here?' I asked Morag when the girl had gone. 'What strange can of worms did I open?'

Either the press or I had created bizarre hysteria in people's reactions.

The Mission

For a while, I was glad my mission had reverted to the plan that I'd marry by the end of the Festival. I was too exhausted to face any more dating or email-writing, and wanted it all to end. The reaction in the streets continued to be a mixture of praise and jeers, and I was back to taking it all in my stride. Everyone I knew had turned into a Jewish mother. 'So are you married yet?' they would ask with Yiddish shrugs.

Walking down one street, I alternated between yes and no answers and managed at least five of each. Sometimes I would answer 'Yes' to the first ten people who asked me and 'No' to the next ten.

Three women offered to marry me for the hell of it. Two were women I'd come to know during the Festival and were offering to help me out of a hole. The third was a very attractive twenty-two-year-old who quite liked the idea of marrying me for an agreed year to thwart the press. We would make appearances on TV and talk about how we had fallen in love. Her career in entertainment would be helped by all the publicity, so we'd both win. Along with these offers I had also received a number of email proposals of marriage from women wanting a marriage licence for citizenship.

I started seeing all these offers as back-up plans. My mission would be a success. I'd show everyone. There was one week left to find my ideal bride and if I didn't find her I'd marry one of these other women making offers. A marriage licence is just a piece of paper. It means whatever you want it to mean. I hadn't come this far and worked this hard to achieve nothing. The press and critics who had scorned me would eat their words.

Nicole and I had kept in contact by email since I received her speed-dating tick. I rang her and arranged a date. She sounded good. She sounded perfect. I now remembered her as perfect. She would be my last date. We would get married.

The Last Week

All the last shows were loose, fun and gratifying. On some nights I had interesting discussions with the audience about dating. I asked how long constitutes a date, and received a number of amusing replies. 'Two hours,' said one man adamantly. 'Fifteen minutes,' said a woman who went on to say that she'd never see anyone for longer than that. If she liked him, she'd see him again and for longer.

'Well, if fifteen minutes can be a date,' I responded, 'how about ten minutes? Or five minutes? One minute, perhaps? If I say hello to you, have we just had a date?' A girl I addressed the question to said, 'No.'

'It depends if it leads somewhere,' said a man.

'Does that mean we can only call it a date in retrospect?' I asked.

'The length of time of a coffee,' said another man.

'Right. Well, if I don't like the look of the girl I'll just ask for a teaspoonful of coffee.'

Offers of wives continued coming my way and I had a growing number of women offering to marry me for a publicity exercise or just for a laugh. One girl had dropped a card off for me at the venue with nice thoughts and a suggestion I contact her back in London.

The Big Issue asked me to write a column. Phil joked with me about the idea of me writing a review of my show and giving myself six stars. I wrote a review that made fun of some of the more inane reviews I'd read, which mostly consisted of utter nonsense. Bless the *Big Issue* editor, who, to my delight, printed the review. Of course, if anyone saw who'd written it they'd realise it was a joke.

Carey Marx – *Marry Me*

It is no coincidence that Carey Marx's name is an anagram of the god Rara Cemyx, whose very name inspired the early Babylonians to drink until they woke up married, often to their own relatives or their sworn enemies, the Greeks. But Marx does not rely on his namesake-heritage for laughs or kudos; he does not need to.

Marx has had a palpably intense few months in his search for a wife. In this autobiographical self-effacing hour he presents us with some of the up and down snippets of an endeavour that nearly killed him. Thank God he survived.

I have given this show six stars and could easily have given it more, but I did not want to be outrageous.

He tells a simple story with simple ideologies in a simple way. Yet the result is anything but simple. It is simply a symbol of the simplicity with which simply being simple can produce complexity in a way that a simpleton simply could not without the complicity of a symposium of the simians who are said to be able to unwittingly simulate something. Love is simple, yet it is too complex to programme into a robot. None of this is addressed in Marx's show, and for good reason. He is more concerned with his pragmatic approach to finding love among the type of people that women happen to be.

An antithesis of a show about finding an ideal enemy as this show is, it often seems to be balancing on the pinhead edge of the precipice of loves-end that overhangs the village of desperate-longing in which many of our kind reside. Some of us just renting and some of us blindly buying more property.

I myself have been on a date with Marx and I gave that six stars, too.

Funny, touching, shocking, educational and ticklish, this show goes where other shows are truly afraid to go. Sure, it left some questions in the air but that is better than leaving them in a locker, and fortunately it kept the answers firmly on the ground and brought condign applause from a mixed-height audience.

Nothing gives me greater pleasure than to recommend this show. I insist that you see it.

Nicole

Nicole came to Edinburgh to see me. It's quite easy to take a girl out on a date during the Festival. There are a few thousand shows to see.

We went to some. The date was excellent. I asked her why she wanted to marry me.

'It will be funny,' she said. 'I've never done anything like this before.'

We were in a bar where the acts hang out. My peripheral vision caught a couple in the corner. I turned and looked at Morag and James laughing at a filthy joke. I knew that it was a filthy joke because it was them. They had announced their engagement the day before. They looked great together.

I bought Nicole another drink and said, 'It would be great if you come to the show tonight.'

The Last Night

On the way to my show, I became a bit light headed and this was helped by copious amounts of alcohol. I rang David and a few friends and told them what I wanted to do that night. They were up for it.

I raced home to do some research with a friend called Jamie, who looked up the pagan festival of Handfasting.

We wrote out some wedding vows based on the traditional Handfast vows.

Jamie arrived for the end of the show to play a drum. My good buddy Stephen came to conduct the ceremony. I announced to my audience that I was going to marry them all. To the best of my knowledge, no one has ever married a whole audience before.

'We are gathered here today to witness the joining of this audience and this performer . . .' Stephen read off the sheet we had thrown together. He introduced the witnesses and told the audience that if anyone knew any just cause why the union should not take place they should keep their silence. We swore on a breadknife. It is supposed to be a ritual knife but a breadknife was all I could find. He had me repeat the vows:

'I, Carey Marx, the performer,

Promise to respect this audience's need to be challenged

Be true to my convictions even if some don't get it

Put the audience above the critics

And get this audience into my gigs for free when in their area if
    possible.

My love will be your mirth when your heart is touched by
sadness.'

Then the audience repeated:

'We promise to always give this performer the benefit of the
doubt

And try our best to laugh with and not at him.

To sleep with him regularly and not say we all have a headache

To drink the blood of a goat if necessary

To not eat loudly or heckle relentlessly during his performances

In sickness and in health

And through good review and bad.'

At this point, Stephen had to make a religious gesture, which he did
but it was difficult to describe. It involved a guttural noise and a quite
threatening wave of the breadknife. Then he said:

'Your love will be your banquet when life's table seems empty,
Your love will be your shining star through the darkest of
nights.'

Then everyone held hands and the person on the front row held a
rope, which we knotted. I held the other end.

'As this knot is tied

So are your lives now bound

So mote it be'

And just like that I was married to an audience for a year and a day. They were a very nice audience, too. I think a couple of them were already married but a performer marrying his audience should transcend such trivial detail.

I had a drink with Nicole afterwards. She seemed relieved.

Later, in the bars the reaction to my marriage was exactly as I had expected. Some people thought it was hilarious and congratulated me. Other people were unimpressed and told me it was a cop-out. I was very happy with myself.

A few hours later, I was extremely drunk. By five in the morning I'd handed out some bottles of champagne and a few boxes of chocolates to people who had helped me during the Festival, and then I staggered off to a party that housemate Matt had told me he'd be at. I had one bottle of champagne and a box of good chocolates left. On the way, people stopped me to ask if I was married. I told them I'd married my audience. I enjoyed all their reactions.

As I walked I smiled at the thought of everything that had happened and felt relieved it had ended. I was still single. But I'd become far better at being single than I'd ever been before. I knew how to get dates easily and I knew how to enjoy them. I'd made a mass of new friends, some of whom I truly treasured. Sticking a cigarette into my mouth, I giggled at the tasks I'd set myself in those hazy, ambitious moments from which my project emanated.

I reached the party but it had finished. Matt and some others were on the street saying that they intended to walk up Arthur's Seat – I don't know if Arthur's Seat is considered a mountain or a hill. Though I'd been to Edinburgh a few times, I'd never climbed it. I thought guiltily about all the things I should be doing and then realised for the first time in months that there were none. So we walked up Arthur's Seat.

We took the steep route. I took the chocolates and champagne with me. I felt quite romantic. I love romance. Romance is a magical thing. It is a thing that is bigger than the sum of its parts. It is a sentence or a gesture that touches another person. I used to think it was something for women and Italians. I used to think it had to be roses and candlelit dinners. But it can be so many things. It can be a gift from a man to a woman. It can be a wink from a friend to a friend. It can be a few words which make someone smile for hours. It can be a night out which makes someone feel valued. It can be organising a surprise genocide for someone.

It can be a man walking up a mountain carrying a box of chocolates and a bottle of champagne to share with whomever he finds at the top.

OK, I did get Matt to put the champagne and chocolates in his backpack for part of the climb, but most of the way up I held them in my outstretched hands, grinning contentedly and stepping carefully.

As I pulled myself over a ridge I reached a decision that I would complete all the tasks I had set myself. Quit smoking for good, master some exciting dishes, learn some romantic poetry, get fit, buy a new wardrobe of clothes and take fighting lessons. I would do it all for me.

Sitting on a rock at the summit, a handful of people were waiting for the sun to rise. They invited us onto their rock. We joined them and looked down over Edinburgh. It was all so far away.

The sun rose big and red. Its arms yawned across the horizon and proclaimed a new day. We all cheered. I popped the champagne and everyone drank from it. We were all joking and laughing.

'So you were the guy who was going to get married,' said one of the group.

'Yup.'

'Did you manage it?' asked another.

'I married my audience.'

They were amused.

I stood up on the rock we were perched on. It was windy but I felt steady.

Standing next to a mountain makes you feel small, I decided. But standing on a mountain makes you feel big.

As we started our descent, a man whose name I wish I could remember crouched on the rock and yelled to me through the wind, 'Marry me?'

I said I'd come back for him.

On the way down I remembered how I'd felt on the Klein Matterhorn in January. This was to be the Year of Bold. Don't ask, don't get. And when you stick your neck out, you might get your head chopped off or someone might put a sweet in your mouth. Both had happened to me many times over. I had a pain in my neck but a nice taste in my mouth. I had definitely done something bold. Yes. It had been a very bold year.

I rang Jenni and apologised for waking her up so early but I knew she'd understand how I felt on this glorious morning. We talked until talking on the phone made me slip several feet, so we said goodbye after arranging to meet again soon.

Was it a hill or a mountain we were going down? I decided it was a mountain. It would be a mountain in the movie. Brad Pitt would be wearing an open-neck tuxedo shirt carrying the box of chocolates and the champagne proud and high. He wouldn't get his friend to carry them part of the way in his backpack. He'd dance up the mountain, and on the summit he'd pop the champagne as the sun rose and everyone around would cheer.

And then he would look down and see people coming up the

mountain. There would be thousands of people. And as they drew closer he'd recognise them all. They were the audience he'd married. They'd all hug on the rock and then he'd go with them all to Cyprus on honeymoon. And on the honeymoon he'd meet the girl of his dreams. But she'd say that he couldn't have her because he was already married to an audience and she was a pagan and took these things very seriously.

Sorry, Brad. Romance can be a fickle thing.

THE ENDING

Home from Edinburgh, I had a few days to complete the book. I worked hard on it, but there was so much to do. Large parts were nonsensical, even to me. There were rants about reporters that went on for several pages. I described climbing Arthur's Seat at the end of the Festival, and thought it might be an idea to end the book there. It starts and finishes on a mountain and leaves the success of the mission in the air. It hadn't been a total disaster. Much had come out of it. Perhaps my wife would read the book and come and find me.

One day from my deadline, Phil said, 'I don't like it.'

'Why not?' I asked. 'I can't think of a better ending, except to say I still might get married.'

'I don't know why I don't like it,' he said.

My deadline passed. I rang the publishers and asked for another couple of weeks. They allowed me the time and invited me to a dinner they were throwing for some of their authors. There were speeches praising the authors. I was the one who hadn't written his book yet. Marketing people asked me anxiously if I was married yet. 'It will really help if you get married.' At first I told them all that I hadn't found a wife yet but was still trying. But I knew the truth. I wasn't trying any more at all. I had two weeks left to write a book. I was spending all my time writing it and, far from finding a wife, I now had no social life whatever. I'd been speaking to Jenni daily, but told her that I would have to see her when the book was in.

The people at Headline are all interesting, intelligent and friendly folk. I was enjoying mixing with them. I had an idea. If I could sell the non-marriage ending to them, to people who had a vested interest in the marriage ending, then surely I could sell it at the end of the book? So I started talking about how it was better that I hadn't married anyone. If I had, it would have been such a predictable ending. Not marrying threw all kinds of questions up into the air. It led to discussion over whether the mission was a total waste of time or not.

'I know five couples who've got engaged since I started my mission and there are a few others who've written to say they're getting married, too,' I told one of the girls. 'I think what the mission did was make people think about marriage and romance, and I've had some effect on people's lives.'

She agreed and we discussed it.

To someone else I explained, 'The mission was a success, just not in the way other people would have liked it to have been. I think I proved it possible to meet your ideal wife over such a short time – the couples who got engaged prove that. I did meet my ideal type, but I was asking for too many things to be in place for her to have been my ideal partner. As well as being my ideal type, she had to be free and willing to marry me in a hurry. And she had to put up with all the insanity I had to put up with. It's better to end the book on that note. I set out to prove it possible and I achieved that. Plus, I came damn close to finding a wife. No, the book should end in the real world. If we learn lessons from our endeavours and achieve something useful, that success should be savoured.'

She agreed.

The next day I had lunch with Phil. 'I need to marry someone,' I told him.

'Yes, you do,' he said. 'I agree with all your arguments over why it was successful, but that's just not an ending.'

I arrived home. Janice was in the kitchen. 'I'm sorry you didn't marry anyone,' she said.

'That's the problem,' I said. 'I'm not. People seem to be feeling sorry for me and I don't feel sorry for myself at all. I had a great year and learnt loads. I just want to be free from all this now, so I can start putting everything I learnt to good use.'

'What will you do?'

'I want to see Jenni for a while. We've got something nice happening and I want to see where it's going. But I want to give it a fair chance without the pressure of forcing it to go somewhere in a hurry. I want to start enjoying the romance. If it doesn't work out I know that at least we'll still be great friends. And I don't mind being single, either, if it comes to that. I want to go out on dates to enjoy them without having to report back to anyone and without an agenda. I think I'll find a wife as a result of this mission in my own relaxed time.'

That night I sat on my bed and made a list of options.

1) Marry Jenni. I think I could talk her into it. We get on fabulously well. But she would be doing it to get me out of a bind. She would be doing it for me and not for us.

2) Marry one of the girls who wanted to marry me for a laugh or for a work permit; we'd have to keep it going for at least a year, but could then divorce. As I examined this option, I wondered why I hadn't done it. The answer was obvious. It was because my view of marriage had changed quite dramatically. I didn't want to marry an asylum seeker or an actress just for show, because it would get in the

way of my finding the real thing. And now I wanted something real because I had touched it, it had touched me, and I remembered how good it felt.

3) Turn gay.

4) Hand in the book with the finale of me marrying the audience, and argue belligerently with anyone who had a problem with that ending.

I stared blankly at the page wishing I could find a real solution so that I could go out enjoying myself. And then, more because I thought five seemed a better number of options than four, I wrote an option five on the page.

5) Fail. I'd originally demanded the right to fail on my mission but I'd demanded it for all the wrong reasons. I'd wanted to be able to fail to prove the task impossible and to justify my stagnant love life. Now failure would allow me to have a love life worth loving. I'd got so wrapped up in proving myself to everyone that I'd totally forgotten about failure as an option. The mission had already failed, but with too much denial. Now I could come clean. I started ringing people and telling them my mission had failed. I set out to find a wife by the end of August, and I failed. No excuses. No provisos, restrictions or qualifications. I failed. Everyone was very happy for me.

The thing that has surprised me most this year is how shy people are about their private lives. That damned embarrassment factor. No one wants to fail or, particularly, to be seen failing. We all want to be winners. I'd come to understand it because my mission had the very result they'd have feared. And I was embarrassed about it. If I'd succeeded, people like the man I was a few months ago wouldn't have been moved. They'd still be just as afraid of not succeeding, maybe even more so. They'd argue that the book and the show made it possible for me, but that kind of thing didn't happen to them. But now I could really do something. For all the people I met this year and for all the people who shared their personal stories and lives with me and their fears of rising above their situations, I would gallantly fail. I would do this for them and I would do this for me. And everyone would see that it really is not such a terrible thing.

I would fail boldly.

Failure is a friend. I even think it is romantic. It is human. Back in March I breezily wrote that failure is sometimes the most effective course of action. Now I actually believe that. Without the failure of attempts at alcohol prohibition we wouldn't be able to get drunk together. Without heart failure, hearts would carry on beating after someone's body was dead – that would be too weird. Without evolution's abundant failures in most of its adaptations and mutations, we wouldn't exist. Without failure to turn up for work, you'd always turn up for work. The Leaning Tower of Pisa was supposed to stand straight, but if it had who would visit it?

I failed to achieve the things on my list that would make me eligible. I failed to finish the book in time for the deadline. And I failed to find a wife. That is it. It is over.

I FAILED.

Now I'm going to go out and have some fun.